The Joshua Principle

Changing the World by Reaching Children and Youth

Mark Hoffman

The Joshua Principle
Changing the World by Reaching Children and Youth

Copyright 2007 by Mark Hoffman

Second Edition Copyright 2010 by Mark Hoffman

Second Edition Revised Copyright 2019 by Mark Hoffman

All Rights Reserved

ISBN: 9781077653597

First published by:
Christian Services Network
P.O. Box 1450
Pine Valley, CA 91962

Unless otherwise indicated, scripture quotations are taken from the New American Standard Bible® (NASB). ©1960, 1962, 1963, 1968, 1971, 1972, 1973, 1975, 1977, 1995 by the Lockman Foundation. Used by permission.

Printed in the United States of America.

For more content from Mark Hoffman, visit www.foothillschurch.org/sermons-archive

Table of Contents

Second Edition Update

I have been very gratified by the response to *The Joshua Principle*. Since its release almost three years ago, I have received many reports of how the principles in this book are being used with great success—not only in this country, but in several foreign countries as well.

At home we have continued to see the fruit and blessing by following these same biblical principles. We continue, as we have for more than 20 years, to see growth and powerful results with the children and youth of our community. Since the release of *The Joshua Principle*, we have continued to add new Bible clubs at local schools and are reaching more children and youth than ever before. As I write this, we are just back from our three summer camps which broke all records for attendance and were life-changing for hundreds of youth. In addition, we recently concluded our annual youth conference with over 2,400 in attendance! The council members and police of our city give testimony of how our outreach ministries have made a huge difference in this difficult city.

How do we do it? We can only do it because of the enthusiastic work of those who have graduated from our youth programs and gone on to become adult leaders themselves.

Our focus on youth and children has fueled the continued growth of our church through evangelism. Our adult membership has grown steadily through our youth and children's ministry, both as we reach their parents through their influence and testimony and also as the young people grow up themselves to assume leadership positions in our church.

Through our efforts to train and disciple youth, we have been able to release young leaders to churches and ministries around our county and across the nation. This year many of our young people planted a new, thriving church.

I enthusiastically encourage you to read this book and see if it doesn't truly reflect God's plan to transform your city as well.

Mark Hoffman

Dedication

To our interns and the hundreds of volunteers at Foothills Christian Church and Schools, Youth Venture Teen Centers and the Sonshine and Higher Ground afterschool clubs, who have caught God's vision and are changing the world by reaching and bringing up the next generation.

Foreword

When Mary Magdalene looked into the empty tomb of our Lord, all she saw was a problem. The body she had come to prepare for burial was missing. She began to weep. Two men who were sitting there (angels actually) asked her, "Woman, why are you weeping?" She replied, "Because they have taken away my Lord, and I do not know where they have laid Him" (John 20: 11-13). She saw but she didn't really see. She saw but she did not perceive.

When John the Apostle looked into that same empty tomb, we read that he saw and believed (John 20:8). Both Mary and John saw the same scene. They both had listened to the same Lord and had heard the same teaching. However, when John looked into the empty tomb he saw what Mary had not; he saw and believed.

Even today people can read the same Bible, claim to follow the same Lord, and yet see very differently. They can look out over the same scene and come to different conclusions. Few things in life are simple and straightforward. Life presents us with seeming contradictions. Everybody must choose their perspective and make their choices in the face of seemingly contradictory evidence.

William Jennings Bryan said that destiny is not a matter of chance, it is a matter of choice; it is not a thing to be waited for, it is a thing to be achieved.[1] The world of today is full of fear and

---

1Bryan, Williams Jennings. Qtd. In "William Jennings Bryan Quotes" (Online). <http://en.thinkexist.com/quotes/william_jennings_bryan/>

confusion. People are uncertain of what to do next. But this presents a moment of great opportunity for people who have vision and understanding. In Daniel, the eleventh chapter, we read that, "The people who know their God will display strength and take action. Those who have insight among the people will give understanding to the many" (Daniel 11:32-33).

What do you see when you look around today? Can you find the great opportunities that are before us? Unless you can, you can't "display strength" or "give understanding to the many." Many people look around today without truly seeing. They see the violence and decay, but they don't see the promise of a better tomorrow. Where is the promise of a better tomorrow? It lies in the potential of the children and teenagers who live all around us. Some people look around at the youth and wring their hands and can only quote the statistics on teen pregnancy, drug use, and school dropout rates. Those people see, but they don't really see.

The only reason we have the largest Sunday school in the world at Metro Ministries is because I saw something, and so I stayed. Others saw the poverty, gangs, and misery, and they left. But we saw something more. We saw the potential of God in the youngsters growing up in Brooklyn and the surrounding communities. And until you can see it too, you haven't really seen.

I am here today because years ago one man could see what others could not. When my mother abandoned me on a street corner, she didn't want me. Neither did anyone else. I sat there for three days, all alone, waiting in vain for her to return. But then one man saw me sitting there and he cared – he cared enough to stop. He cared enough to send me to church camp at his expense because he saw what others couldn't see. Without his vision Metro Ministries would never exist.

What do you see? What is your level of faith and commitment when you look around at the young people of your church or your city? It can be difficult to see with vision, and even more difficult to see that vision through to fulfillment. It will involve overcoming discouragement and fatigue. But the ability to finish is only achieved when your commitment outweighs your emotions.

Are you willing to take a stand for a generation that is growing up all around us? Are you willing to do more for that generation than was ever done for us? Are you willing to lay down your life to reach that generation? If we don't do it, no one else will. Just what do you see when you look around? How do you see the place, importance and potential of ministry to children and youth?

In this book, my friend Mark Hoffman will help you to see as you ought to see. He will help you to have insight, understanding, and the faith and conviction to take action. I have been to Mark's church many times and have seen for myself how they are changing their world through reaching the generation that is growing up around them. Their approach to ministry is radical in that they have searched out the Scriptures for their philosophy and strategies rather than just following whatever is the latest rage. The principles in this book are transferable to any setting because they are the principles of the Bible. I challenge you to read this book and see how these foundational truths will help you to change your world.

Bill Wilson
Metro Ministries, New York City

x

Introduction

Our church averages just under 2,400 people in weekend worship service attendance. *Yet every week we average more than 5,000 children and youth in attendance at our various ministries and outreaches.* These are not just "touches" but significant ministry encounters. The obvious question that comes to a person's mind upon hearing this is, "How?" But perhaps an even more important question is, "Why?"

Answering the "How" is easy. We are able to reach this many children and youth each week through operating two Christian schools, twenty-four onsite afterschool Christian clubs at area public schools, four community teen centers, bus routes, apartment visitations, mentoring programs as well as church youth groups, small groups, Sunday school, and various other camps and programs. We do this with a small number of staff and a huge army of volunteers.

Answering the "Why" is more significant. We can only accomplish this year in and year out because of some convictions that God has put deep within our hearts. These convictions all arise out of our understanding of the Bible and the purposes of God revealed there. In it God shows forth His plan of bringing forth blessing and increase through generational transfer. In other words, as the older generation invests in the younger, both generations receive blessing and increase and God's Kingdom advances.

This book was written to help you understand this great truth. The principles outlined in this book will enrich your life and enlarge your effectiveness for Jesus and His Kingdom. These principles will also operate on the level of family and church.

The convictions and principles outlined in this book will work for any church of any size. I know this because they have worked for us ever since we were very small. It is not wise to try to copy other churches' methods, but it is wise to follow the Bible's principles.

The community we serve is the east San Diego County area. It is a very ethnically and economically diverse area of about 250,000 people. The city we are located in, El Cajon, California, is a city of about 90,000 and is the fifth-fastest ethnically transitioning city in all of California. It has long been a national center of drug production and has developed a very serious gang problem. It is not an area where many people come to plant churches.

Despite all these challenges, our ministry to youth and children has continued to grow, and we have seen neighborhoods change. Our vision remains to change our community and the larger world by reaching and bringing up the next generation.

These principles will also work in any family. I also know this because they worked in my family and that of many others I have witnessed. They work because they are God's principles.

My prayer is that you will pray through this book and ask God what it means for you, your family, and your church. May God give rich blessings to you and your children through this book.

1

The Joshua Principle

Joshua was Israel's great general and leader following the death of Moses. It was under his leadership that Israel took and possessed the Promised Land. This was the land that God had promised to Abraham, almost six centuries earlier, as an inheritance for his descendants. The land was known as Canaan. It was so rich and fertile that the Bible described it as "a land flowing with milk and honey" (Exodus 3:8). Moreover, it was a land that was already well developed with vineyards, wells, roads, and cities. The land, however, was not empty. It was fully populated by fierce people who lived in great walled and fortified cities. The land would not be gained except through great determination and pitched warfare.

Joshua led Israel in great victories, beginning with the famous Battle of Jericho. No king or city could stand before the army of Israel. The task of gaining the entire land of Canaan was a huge one and would require about twenty-five years (Exodus 23:28-29; Deuteronomy 7:22). But through it all Israel stayed strong and remained faithful, and God fought on Israel's side so that near the end of Joshua's life it could be said that Israel had full victory.

So the Lord gave Israel all the land which He had sworn to give to their fathers, and they possessed it and lived in it. And the Lord gave them rest on every side, according to all that He had sworn to their fathers, and no one of all their enemies stood before them; the Lord gave all their enemies into their hand. Not one of the good promises which the Lord had made to the house of Israel failed; all came to pass.

Joshua 21:43-45

What a glorious accomplishment. This was certainly one of the greatest high water marks in all of Israel's history. Israel had inherited the fullness of the promises that God had given them. Through God, Joshua had *finally* gained the victory. I say finally because we must remember that this was not his first attempt at taking the Promised Land. Joshua had been there 40 years earlier with Moses. He had come among the generation fresh from the exodus out of Egypt.

This was the generation that had seen God's great plagues upon the Egyptians as well as seeing the Egyptian army drowned in the Red Sea. They had been led by the pillar of fire by night and the pillar of cloud by day. They had drunk water from a rock and had defeated the Amalekites. Moses was their leader and Joshua was second in command under Moses and was also their greatest general (Exodus 17:9-10, 13). Yet when they came to the border of the Promised Land, they resisted Moses' and Joshua's leadership, and they failed to enter.

Joshua's generation was not prepared to enter. They had been raised in slavery and continued to think like slaves. They complained when faced with any difficulties (Numbers 11:1), were critical of their leaders (Numbers 12:1), and were unbelieving of God's ability to bring His promise to pass in their lives (Numbers 13:31). They did not see themselves as a people made great because their God was great. They were overwhelmed and intimidated by their human adversaries and the challenges of mastering a new land. Worst of all, whenever challenges would come,

14

they always wanted to go back to the false security of slavery in Egypt.

All of this came to a tragic head as they camped on the border of the Promised Land. Joshua had been one of the twelve spies that had been sent in to spy out the land. As you may remember, ten of the twelve spies came back with a bad report.

But the men who had gone up with him said, "We are not able to go up against the people, for they are too strong for us." So they gave out to the sons of Israel a bad report of the land which they had spied out, saying, "The land through which we have gone, in spying it out, is a land that devours its inhabitants; and all the people whom we saw in it are men of great size. There also we saw the Nephilim (the sons of Anak are part of the Nephilim); and we became like grasshoppers in or own sight, and so we were in their sight."'

Numbers 13:31-33

What an incredible statement! They saw themselves as grasshoppers, and despite Joshua's and Caleb's assertions that God was able and would give them the land, they were afraid and refused to enter. A little later they said:

"Would that we had died in the land of Egypt! Or would that we had died in this wilderness! Why is the Lord bringing us into this land, to fall by the sword? Our wives and our little ones will become plunder; would it not be better for us to return to Egypt?" So they said to one another, "Let us appoint a leader and return to Egypt."

Numbers 14:2-4

Then the people prepared to kill Moses, Joshua, and Caleb with stones. God became very angry and His response was swift.

Of the twelve spies, the ten who gave the bad report died suddenly, and only Joshua and Caleb were left alive (Numbers 14:37-38). Then God addressed the whole congregation.

"As I live," says the Lord, "just as you have spoken in My hearing, so I will surely do to you; your corpses shall fall in this wilderness, even all your numbered men, according to your complete number from twenty years old and upwards, who have grumbled against Me. Surely you shall not come into the land in which I swore to settle you, except Caleb the son of Jephunneh and Joshua the son of Nun. Your children, however, whom you said would become a prey – I will bring them in, and they will know the land which you have rejected."
Numbers 14:28-29, 31

What a terrible judgment! That generation would not enter the land. They would not realize their destiny or enjoy the fulfillment of God's promises to them. The glorious exodus from Egypt would not be followed by an equally glorious gaining of the Promised Land but rather a life of wandering around the wilderness. Only two from that generation could fulfill their purpose and receive everything that God had promised. Only Joshua and Caleb could enter the land. And they would do so, *only if* they gave themselves to training up the next generation.

They must raise up a generation that didn't think like slaves, that didn't see themselves as grasshoppers serving a grasshopper God. They must raise up a generation who grew up in freedom from childhood and who wouldn't want to run back to the security of slavery whenever they felt threatened. They must train up such a generation, for it would only be with such a people that they themselves could gain the land.

This, then, is the Joshua Principle. *We can only fully gain*

16

1: The Joshua Principle

the promises of God through focusing on training up the next generation.

God is a generational God. He makes promises that are multi-generational. These promises are gained when the generations work together and are lost when the generations become estranged (Malachi 4:5-6). This is illustrated everywhere in Scripture.

- Adam and Eve sinned but were promised deliverance and victory over Satan through an offspring (Genesis 3:15).

- Noah built an ark and brought his sons and their wives into it. Through his sons the world was repopulated (Genesis 9:1).

- Abraham was called by God and given great promises that through *his descendants* all mankind would be blessed (Genesis 12:1-3; 13:14-16).

- Moses brought the people out of Egypt, but he trained up Joshua to bring them into the Promised Land (Deuteronomy 3:28).

- King David collected the materials and treasures for the temple, but his son Solomon built it (1 Kings 8:17-20).

- God the Father effected salvation for all mankind through sending His Son (John 3:16-17).

- The apostle Paul ministered widely but was careful to train up younger men like Timothy and Titus, whom he referred to as sons in the faith (2 Timothy 1:2, 13-14; 2:1-2; Titus 1:4).

In the same way, Jesus built with this principle in mind. He looked outside the current generation of leadership and chose outsiders. He did not try to change what already was but said, rather, that new wine required a new wine skin (Mark 2:22). Jesus built in light of what would come after Him. He built into the lives of twelve successors who would in turn build upon the foundation that He laid.

Just like Joshua, we, too, have great promises before us. But we will only fully realize these promises if we give ourselves to loving and training up the generation under us. If you are a parent, realize that your greatest opportunity for happiness in the future is not by working directly for that happiness but rather by sacrificing to raise up godly children. If you succeed in doing this, your children and grandchildren will bring you your greatest chance for future happiness and future blessing. If you fail due to carelessness, neglect or selfishness on your part, you will have little chance for happiness in the future.

If you are a pastor or leader, understand that your greatest effectiveness will be through raising up those who can join and follow you in being productive. If you focus only on adding con-verts, you will never be able to multiply. Only by bringing spiri-tual sons and daughters to maturity can you begin to see multi-plication take place. And multiplication will soon outdistance what you can do by addition.

If you care about the future that you will one day have to live in, then you must learn the Joshua Principle. Too often in the church we have sought for easy, quick fixes to the problem of our culture, but we have continued to see our culture decline. There are no quick fixes. Only by investing in the next generation can you and I see the world we hope for rather than the world we dread. This book is written with the conviction that the Joshua Principle will still work today even as it has in the past. It is also written with the hope that you will become like Joshua.

This book is not just a theoretical book. Rather, it is a record of how the Joshua Principle is working in one church and in one community. It is a record of how a church can change a community and change the future once it realizes that the future belongs to the children.

The greatest power for good and the only hope for the future is the Kingdom of God, and Jesus said that it belongs to the children (Mark 10:14).

The Joshua Principle

2

The Day Jesus Went to Church

J esus stood at the entrance to the courtyard of the great temple in Jerusalem and looked in. He had traveled to Jerusalem to be there in time for the week-long Passover Feast. Before Him lay the Court of the Gentiles, the first of three great outer courts that surrounded the temple building itself. It was a bustle of activity on that day. His sharp eyes took it all in.

Those who came to the temple that day to offer sacrifices, pay vows, or conduct business may have thought that it looked like any other day, but it wasn't. It was to be a very different kind of day. It was the day Jesus came to church.

Fast forward 2000 years and imagine that this week Jesus visited earth in a human body for a day. Imagine that He woke up this Sunday morning in your city. Would He go to church? Of course, He would. The Bible tells us that it was His habit to go the local synagogue each Sabbath in every town He visited (Luke 4:16).

Here's a tougher question: Which church in your city would Jesus go to? What does Jesus look for and value in a church? At which church would He want to spend Sunday morning?

Let's take it one step further. Imagine that Jesus became the pastor of the average church in your community for one year. In fact, imagine that He became the pastor of *your* church for one year. Would He make changes? What kind of changes would He make in the operation of your church?

Finally, one last question to ponder. Would most Christians in your community want to go to the church after Jesus changed it to be just what He wanted?

Let's go back to the first century. The day that Jesus went to church was a typical day at the temple. Everything was going as planned. It was all happening just the way the priests and temple insiders had set it up, just the way they wanted it.

The Insiders

The moneychangers were doing a brisk business. They had a sweet racket going with the temple priests. Every male Jew had to pay a yearly temple tax of half a shekel for the upkeep of the temple (this was equal to about two days wages for the average laborer). The priests ruled, however, that people could not use the ordinary money that circulated in society to pay the tax, but rather they must pay it using a special approved currency, available only at the temple. You could only exchange your money for this special currency at the temple and for a substantial fee, which the moneychangers shared with the priests.

The animal sellers were also busy selling the animals which would be used in sacrifices. Now, the Law stated that you could buy your sacrificial animal anywhere. You could even bring one from home. The Law did state that it had to be a healthy, valuable animal...or as the Law put it, without "blemish," (Deuteronomy 17:1). God wants us to give Him our best, not our discards. In order to ensure that people were bringing true sacrifices, and not

22

just sick or defective animals, the priests had to examine each animal. And this is where the temple insiders were able to turn it to their advantage. They could find something wrong with nearly any animal. After all, like people, there are no flawless or perfect animals. The only safe bet was to buy one of the overpriced pre-approved animals. This also proved to be a cozy deal for the priests and animal sellers.

In other words, on the day Jesus went to church, everything was set up for the benefit and comfort of the insiders. They had gotten it just the way that they wanted it, but they had forgotten one thing. The temple belonged to God. It was to serve His purposes and accomplish His agenda.

What was worse is that this was all happening in the Court of the Gentiles. This is the only place in the temple precincts in which non-Jews were allowed. Here people from all the nations could be found praying and seeking the famous God of the Jews who had sent the prophets and given the magnificent Law of Moses, which was respected around the world. Actually, I should say that they attempted to pray and seek God amidst all the buying and selling and braying of animals.

This is what was happening on the day that Jesus went to church. Most of you probably remember how that visit went.

And Jesus entered the temple and drove out all those who were buying and selling in the temple, and over-turned the tables of the money changers and the seats of those who were selling doves. And He said to them, "It is written, 'MY HOUSE SHALL BE CALLED A HOUSE OF PRAYER'; but you are making it a ROBBERS' DEN." And the blind and the lame came to Him in the

*temple, and He healed them. But when the chief priests
and the scribes saw the wonderful things that He had
done, and the children who were shouting in the temple,
"Hosanna to the Son of David," they became indignant
and said to Him, "Do You hear what these children are
saying?" And Jesus said to them, "Yes; have you never
read, 'OUT OF THE MOUTH OF INFANTS AND
NURSING BABIES YOU HAVE PREPARED PRAISE
FOR YOURSELF'?" And He left them and went out of
the city to Bethany, and spent the night there.*

Matthew 21:12-17

When Jesus went to church that day, the temple insiders
were inside and the outsiders were outside. The insiders were on
the inside running the show. They were conducting business,
accomplishing their desire, and furthering their agenda. After
Jesus came they were on the outside. This is referred to by
theologians as "the cleansing of the temple." But the story tells
us more than just what Jesus removed from the temple. It also
tells us what He put in their place. Look carefully again at the
story.

*And the blind and the lame came to Him in the
temple...and the children who were shouting in the
temple, "Hosanna to the Son of David."*

Matthew 21:14-15

On the day that Jesus cleansed and emptied the temple, what
did He fill the temple with? He filled it with the blind, lame, and
hurting who were coming to Him to be healed, and He filled it with
children shouting and worshiping out of joy at finding Jesus the
Messiah. Instead of the business and clever plans of men there was
true worship and heartfelt prayer. When Jesus left that day He was
pleased. Church, on that day at least, had become what He wanted
it to be.

Filled With Children

Perhaps the most noteworthy change that day was that the temple was filled with children and young people running and shouting with joy. It was, after all, the one thing that the Pharisees made special note of and complained about (verse 15).

This is how Jesus wants His churches today. He wants them full of children and young people joyfully worshiping and following their Savior. He wants His churches overflowing with children and youth who are excited about church, loving every minute of it. And He wants them loving church for the right reason. Not because of great entertainment but because they are finding and encountering Jesus there.

These are the churches that Jesus seeks. These are the ones that experience His presence in their meetings, the ones that welcome the blind, lame, and hurting, and the ones that go out of their way to reach out and bring in the children and youth and make church a place that they want to be.

However, when we look at much of the current church scene, we see that the children and youth are often missing. Those youth who are there are often sullen and bored, just marking time until they can leave. What have we done to Jesus' church?

The Joshua Principle

3

To Whom Does the Kingdom Belong?

A recent survey revealed that one-third of all thirteen-year-olds who regularly attend church will drop out by the time they are eighteen[1]. Another big drop will occur as young people leave home and move out on their own.

How can we explain the fact that so many young people sit in churches unaffected, bored and alienated, just waiting for their chance to drop out? After all, as we saw from the previous chapter, on the day that Jesus visited the temple, the children and youth were especially noted for their joyful, exuberant worship of Jesus.

I can tell you after nearly thirty years of ministering to children and youth of all backgrounds that they still exhibit a deep hunger and interest for Jesus and the message of the Bible. In fact, *research today confirms that children between the ages of eight to thirteen are the greatest spiritual seekers in the world.* Consider the following startling statistics. The widely respected pollster and researcher George Barna has discovered that while ten to twelve year olds account for only 4 percent of the population, it is the age range at which over one quarter of all believers made their decision to follow Christ. In fact, if you extend the period to the ages of eight to

---

[1] George Barna, *Generation Next* (Ventura: Regal Books, 1995), 87.

thirteen, you find that almost 50 percent of all Christians today made their decision for Christ while in that age group[2].

If a person does not make a decision for Christ by the time they graduate from junior high school, chances are great that they never will. About 4 percent of non-Christians who enter high school as freshman will make a decision for Christ by the time they graduate. If we fail to reach them by high school, the odds of reaching them drops sharply. Of those who graduate from high school without becoming a Christian, only 6 percent will make a decision for Christ before they die.

The implications of these facts are as obvious as they are profound. We must focus our evangelism on children and young adolescents. It's when people have the best chance of accepting Christ.

The Creator's Plan

How are we to understand all of this? We must remember that there are certain critical periods in human development where certain developmental issues must be encountered. These periods are optimal windows when all the factors come together for us to learn certain skills and gain understanding that will allow us to become healthy, productive adults. If we miss these optimal windows then later we will be at a great disadvantage in trying to compensate. For example, the ages of infancy to fifteen months are a critical time when an infant must learn trust and bonding. It is essential that a baby is held and cuddled during this period. Studies have proven that when babies are not cuddled and held, they will not develop

---

[2]Barna 78-79.

the ability to bond and will grow up having a very hard time being able to trust people or develop empathy with others.

In the same way, toddlers (one-to three-year-olds) must learn initiative and independence. They must be given stimulation that excites their imagination and opportunities to explore. Likewise the preschool and kindergarten years are when we learn social skills and how to interact with others. During this period, children who are isolated from others, especially peers, must struggle harder later in life to develop social skills and may always struggle in social situations. There are additional developmental windows I could cite as well.

It seems the Creator set the period of time of ten to twelve years old—some people a little earlier, some a little later—as the most important period in a person's spiritual development and walk with God. Lisa Miller of Columbia University went so far as to say, "A search for spiritual relationship with the Creator may be an inherent development process in adolescence."[3]

All the conditions that make for spiritual hunger and searching seem to come together at this point. Intellectually, the brain, for the first time, develops the capacity for abstract reasoning and for exploring what they believe and why, socially they are moving toward greater independence from the family. They are seeking where they belong and are developing their own identity and personal code to live by. Young adolescents are trying to find their first answers to the great questions of life.

---

[3] Josh McDowell, *Josh McDowell's Personal Notes on Religion*, http://www.josh.org/notes/file/internet13-religion.pdf (May 11, 2007).

In short, they are openhearted, inquisitive, pliable, trusting, and responsive. These are the very preconditions necessary for receiving the Kingdom of God. However, the window of opportunity doesn't last forever. By age thirteen or fourteen most people have begun to settle on their answers to the great questions of life and have chosen their identity and their path for life. Every year they become less likely to change.

Facts show that if a person fails to receive Christ as Savior during this childhood period, it's unlikely that person ever will unless some overwhelming event reproduces these childlike conditions later in their life. Usually when an adult does come to Christ it's following some tragic event that humbles them and causes them to become teachable and open to new answers. Jesus Himself made this point clear when He told some adults:

> *Truly I say to you, unless you are converted and become like children, you will not enter the kingdom of Heaven.*
> Matthew 18:3 (see also Mark 10:15 & Luke 18:17)

Research indicates that a person's basic spiritual and moral views and beliefs are largely formed by the time they're thirteen. After they become adults, unless they undergo some life-shaking, life-changing experience that causes them to "become like children," they will not change their views or beliefs. Researcher George Barna has stated that in the great majority of cases, "…what you believe by the time you are thirteen is what you will die believing."[4]

The great tragedy in America is that most young people arrive at age thirteen or fourteen having settled on their answers and

---

[4]George Barna, *Research Shows That Spiritual Maturity Process Should Start at a Young Age,* http://www.barna.org/FlexPage.aspx?Page=BarnaUpdate&BarnaUpdateID=153 (May 11, 2007).

chosen their life's path without anyone teaching them the Bible or introducing them to the love of the Savior. No one is bringing them to church, and they certainly don't hear about it in school.

It would seem obvious that if we want to see people come to Christ, we must follow our Creator's plan. It makes far more sense to put our best efforts in targeting children and adolescents who by design are the greatest of all spiritual seekers, than to wait and hope that some unforeseen life event will reproduce those same childlike conditions later in their lives so that we can reach them then.

That might seem obvious; however, it is equally obvious that only a tiny fraction of churches understand and practice this strategy. The great bulk of churches spend their best efforts and resources ministering and reaching out to people eighteen and over.

Jesus attracted children like bees to honey, and He welcomed them to Himself. This dynamic is still true today. *In all my nearly thirty years of ministry to people of all ages I can say emphatically that nothing is more natural than watching a child or adolescent young person come to Christ.* Of all the many things I have done in ministry, the single easiest thing is to lead a child or youth to accept Jesus as their Lord and Savior. This is why, even now, as a senior pastor of a large church I continue to devote much of my time and energy to minister to young people in these strategic years.

An Example

Recently my brother-in-law, Jim, who is also a staff pastor, told me of an experience that he had about a month earlier. A ten-year-old boy who had just moved in next door came to see Jim's youngest son. His son was not home, but the boy sort of followed Jim around the yard as Jim was doing a few chores. Jim was cutting back overgrowth using a machete, and since the boy was being somewhat of a pest and Jim was hoping to keep him occupied, he offered the boy a machete to help him. As they began work, the youngster asked Jim what he did for a living. Jim replied that he was a pastor and that his job was to tell people about Jesus. The boy exclaimed, "No way!"

"Yes, it's true," Jim said. "In fact, you can ask me questions about God or the Bible, and I will prove it to you."

The boy asked a number of questions, which Jim answered without much thought or enthusiasm. He had his back to the boy, never taking his attention away from the task at hand, which was trimming back the overgrowth. The talk continued on about God, angels, and the Bible. When the subject of the devil came up the boy said, "Well, if the devil came here I would take this machete to him."

Jim answered, "No the devil is too smart and too strong for a person until they ask Jesus to come into their heart and be their Savior and Lord."

"How does a person ask Jesus into their heart?" the boy asked.

Jim gave him a brief answer and kept working, but a few moments later he heard the boy's small voice behind him, "Tell me again how you do it." Jim turned around to see that his young neighbor had dropped his machete and was down on his knees with his eyes closed and his hands folded in prayer. Jim walked over and led him in the sinner's prayer. Since that day the boy has joined Jim's family in their family devotions, attends Sunday school and midweek children's meetings every week, tells people about Jesus, and those around him have noticed the changes in his young life.

Jim was amazed. He had no idea that leading someone to Christ could happen so easily. But remember, this is how the Creator designed it. It's true, of course, that there will have to be years of patient discipling and coaching if that youngster is to become an overcoming adult Christian. But make no mistake, an encounter with God at that age can determine the rest of a person's life and change the destiny of their descendants.

The Right Focus

It's no accident that we have only one story about Jesus between His birth narratives and His baptism under John the Baptist at age thirty. The only account we have is the story of Jesus at the temple at age twelve. This account is included because it was the most significant event in the life of Jesus up until the events of His baptism and subsequent temptation in the wilderness. In this, Jesus is like so many other adolescents. He had reached the age of spiritual discovery and growth.

If all this is true, how is it that the church has not fared better in our ministry to children and youth? How is it that so few of our strategies, efforts, and resources are focused on reaching this age group? It's reported that four out of every ten people ministered to during the week are children and youth and yet only 12 percent of ministry dollars are spent on them.[5] Further, children's and youth pastors are paid significantly less than any other staff

---

[5]http://www.barna.org/FlexPage.aspx?Page=BarnaUpdate&BarnaUpdateID=153

pastoral position. For instance, the average pay annually for youth or children's pastors is 20 percent less than the annual pay for any other associate pastor.[6]

The reason is the same as in the time of Jesus. In Matthew 19 children are being brought to Jesus:

> *Then some children were brought to Him so that He might lay His hands on them and pray; and the disciples rebuked them. But Jesus said, "Let the children alone and do not hinder them from coming to Me; for the kingdom of heaven belongs to such as these." After laying His hands on them, He departed from there.*
> Matthew 19:13-15

The disciples put up a barrier to keep the children from coming to Jesus. Too often churches are like the disciples. Caught up in wrong agendas, personal preferences, and carnal reasoning, we often hinder children and youth from coming to Christ rather than truly helping them. We build beautiful buildings and then feel we must protect them from children. We design programs and services that appeal to adults but not to young people. We hold tightly to that which appeals to us and resist change. We give little support or prestige to those who minister to children and youth. And worst of all, many adults criticize and scold children and youth for simply being themselves. We require that they dress up, sit still, and be quiet. We require them to act like little adults. Most churches are made to appeal to adults and not to kids. *But Jesus never said that children had to act like adults in order to enter the Kingdom; He said we had to become like them.* He rebuked the disciples for putting up barriers that made it harder for the children to come (Matthew 18:3).

---

[6]James F Cobble, Jr., D.Min., Church Law and Tax Report, 2006 Compensation Handbook for Church Staff, (Matthews: Christian Ministry Resources, 2005) 33.

In shielding Jesus from the children, the disciples no doubt thought that they were being wise. After all, children have no money or power. What can they contribute? They are the most unimportant of all. It's easy to undervalue children and youth. The disciples felt that they should protect Jesus and help Him reserve His energy for meeting more important people, like rabbis and synagogue officials. Those were the people who could pay the bills and really advance Jesus' cause *now*. Plus, the twelve disciples didn't like all the noise and commotion the children brought with them (not to mention how they seemed to break everything in sight).

In their human reasoning, they failed to understand the Kingdom of God does not belong to the rich and powerful. Jesus said it belongs to the children. That is, they enter and gain it most easily. If we can reach people while they are children, it will be their best chance ever to gain the Kingdom. If we truly care about souls we must put our best efforts and finances here. The future of the Kingdom in America is not in the hands of the rich and powerful but in the hands of children. If we reach them today, then tomorrow's churches will be strong. In their salvation lies our salvation.

Jesus said that we must learn from children. Unless you are surrounded by children coming to Christ, unless you witness firsthand their excitement, passion and simple faith, you will soon lose your way. Just as there are things that children and adolescents must depend upon adults for and look to adults as models, so there are things which adults can only learn and remember by watching children and youth.

I have seen for myself how adults are renewed and kept at a high level of joy and zeal for Jesus because of their own ministry to children and youth. I have seen many coldhearted and crusted over Christians re-energized by the enthusiasm and simple faith of young people. I have also witnessed how churches without the presence of children and youth become spiritually dead, petty, and divided. They argue about power, politics, architecture and what color to make the new carpet, all the time unaware that what their heart aches for is the presence of our King and His Kingdom.

But Jesus said, "Let the children alone, and do not hinder them from coming to Me; for the kingdom of heaven belongs to such as these."

Matthew 19:14

What did Jesus mean by saying that the kingdom of heaven belongs to children? I believe that He meant that children (eight to thirteen years-olds especially) enter and gain the kingdom most easily. *What is very hard for an adult comes easily for a young adolescent because of where they are in the Creator's plan of human development.* It's God's time table. It's spiritually the most strategic time in people's lives. It's their best chance to accept Jesus as Savior and enter His Kingdom. For this reason, Jesus promises to severely punish anyone who stumbles or leads astray anyone who is coming to Christ during this most strategic time.

But whoever causes one of these little ones who believe in Me to stumble, it would be better for him to have a heavy millstone hung around his neck, and to be drowned in the depth of the sea.

Matthew 18:6

On the other hand, Jesus promises to reward and honor those who help these young ones to come to Him during this most opportune time. In the verse just before the one cited above Jesus said:

And whoever receives one such child in My Name receives Me.

Matthew 18:5

36

Many people have marveled at the wonderful presence of Jesus that pervades our church meetings. Why, they wonder, does Jesus seem so real and near at our services compared to what they have experienced at so many other churches they have attended? Is it the worship songs that we sing? Is it the way that we preach? Just what is our secret?

I do not pretend to know all the ways of God, nor do we want to take credit for God's blessings that He freely gives. But I do know this; Jesus said that when you receive a child for the sake of Jesus, then you receive Him. I tell people that Jesus is here because He rode over on the bikes and skateboards of our neighborhood kids. He rode over on our Sunday school buses. He got off those same buses and came in the front door with them. This is the best answer I have.

The Joshua Principle

4

The Divine Priority

You seem to hear it everywhere. You hear it at ball games, school assemblies, and city council meetings. It seems that everyone knows it by heart. I'm speaking of the pledge of allegiance. This pledge is one of the things that give us our identity as a nation and ties us all together.

Israel also had such a pledge or creed that gave them their national identity. It was one that all Israelites had committed to memory and recited often in their gatherings. This creed is contained in Deuteronomy 6:4-7. It told them what was most important in life and what God required of them above all. Today we know it as the *Shema,* which comes from the first Hebrew word in that pledge or creed meaning *"hear."* It was considered the most important prayer in the Jewish religion, and Jews had to stand while they recited it. Even today, it's the first prayer that a Jewish child is taught to say. It's the last words a Jew says prior to death.

> *Hear, O Israel! The LORD is our God, the LORD is one!*
> *You shall love the LORD your God with all your heart and*
> *with all your soul and with all your might. These words,*
> *which I am commanding you today, shall be on your heart.*
> *You shall teach them diligently to your sons and shall talk*
> *of them when you sit in your house and when you walk by*
> *the way and when you lie down and when you rise up.*
> Deuteronomy 6:4-7

Here we can see that our primary duty before God is plainly spelled out. As people in covenant with God we have two all important covenant responsibilities.

First, we are to love God with all our being and reverence His Word in our heart.

Second, we are to see that we impart this same covenant, with its divine directions and stipulations, to our children.

We can have no higher priorities than these. We can fail other places, but we can't fail here and be in covenant with God. The primary agenda for every Christian family and every Christian church must be to accomplish these two things. Any church that is not first and foremost about these two things is off the mark. Even trying to win the lost cannot take precedence over these two priorities.

Unfortunately, when it comes down to actual practice, we, as families and churches, often fall short. Many Christian families never have family devotions and seldom pray together. In addition, many Christian parents are not careful about seeing that their children get a Christian worldview. Instead we just drop our kids off at the local schoolhouse door to uncritically absorb whatever is being taught. Often we allow our kids almost unfiltered access to popular media, which ceaselessly undermines God's Word in our children's hearts.

Likewise, our churches often relegate the ministry to children and youth to a secondary status. In most churches it's clearly not a budget priority, and apparently not much thought and attention is given to it. Few senior pastors put much energy into it; they ignore it unless there is a problem that must be addressed.

Our Wonderful Promise

When we do take seriously our covenant responsibility to transmit our sincere faith and raise our children in the Word of God, we receive a wonderful promise.

Train up a child in the way he should go, even when he is old he will not depart from it.

Proverbs 22:6

To *"train up"* means a purposeful strategy to train that child according to God's truth and plan. It assumes that you know *"the way he should go."* This is very different from the largely non-directional, permissive parenting that is so popular in our culture today, which is championed by the so-called experts. In this view children are born naturally good and wise. We need only encourage them, help build their self-esteem, and allow them to clarify their own values and find what works best for them. Without belaboring this point, I hope you realize that this approach is radically opposed to what the Bible teaches and therefore has had disastrous results.

Foolishness is bound up in the heart of a child; the rod of discipline will remove it far from him.

Proverbs 22:15

The rod and reproof give wisdom, but a child who gets his own way brings shame to his mother.

Proverbs 29:15

We cannot claim the wonderful promise of Proverbs 22:6 if we, even subconsciously, accept the modern, humanistic notions of child-raising. We, as parents and churches, must firmly reject the basic assumptions of modern parenting and comprehensively replace it with biblical assumptions and strategies. The key to successful godly children is biblical training and discipline, not building their self-esteem.

41

We must reject the lie that parents are not competent to raise their children but should instead yield to an army of "specialists." God has entrusted the raising of the next generation to parents, not the government or so-called "mental health experts" or educators with secular, humanistic assumptions and methods. God will equip and assist parents through His Word and Spirit to be successful in what He has called them to do. This is God's plan, so He will honor it. As a parent He will "back your act." The church, which is the larger expression of the Christian family, must do whatever is helpful and necessary to assist parents in their responsibility. *The first level of a church's ministry to youth should be to offer parenting classes and mentoring for their parents.*

The wonderful promise that our children "will not depart" from the Lord's way is only given to those who "train up a child in the way he should go." Concerning this promise contained in Proverbs 22:6, allow me to quote from my book, *On Earth as It Is in Heaven*:

"The word *'hanak,'* translated 'train up,' is elsewhere used for dedicating a temple or house (Deuteronomy 20:5; 1 Kings 8:63). In fact, this is its primary usage. It means to 'set apart.' A child is to be 'set apart' to the Lord by the training and education he or she receives. A secondary meaning is to 'fill the hand.' So it also emphasizes that this training must be comprehensive, literally 'filling' the child with God's truth and ways. Countering an entire week's worth of humanistic instruction and training with a couple of hours of church on Sunday does not qualify one to claim this promise with any confidence."[7]

[7]Mark Hoffman, *On Earth as It Is in Heaven* (El Cajon: CSN Books, 2003) 190.

I was raised in a Lutheran church. Lutherans enroll their children in Confirmation Class during the seventh and eighth grade years. At the conclusion of this class they are "confirmed" as full church members during a Sunday morning service. Following this there is a class picture taken. At the church where I attended, they would take these class pictures and display them on the fellowship hall wall. You could see every class picture there since the church was founded some thirty years earlier.

I remember looking at the pictures on that wall one day when I was twenty-three. I especially studied my own graduating class and those for a period of three years before and after my own. These were the kids and families that I knew best. I was shocked when I realized that about 80 percent of those kids were no longer involved in any church.

Had God's promise failed? Of course not. God's Word never fails! His promises are always true and sure. Only one other answer was possible. The church and the parents had failed to fulfill the covenant requirement to "train up" their children. They had instead allowed the traditions of the culture around them to a form their child's heart and mind instead of the Word of God.

A Parent's Responsibility

Every parent must honestly ask themselves:

- "Am I truly living in covenant with God? Have I made the two covenant stipulations of Deuteronomy 6:4-7 my highest priorities in life?"

- "Am I setting an example for my own children by loving God with all my heart and with all my soul and with all my

43

might, or do I give the best of my efforts, thoughts and enthusiasms to pursuing things which are valued and idolized by my culture?"

- "Have I dealt with the pain of past hurts and disappointments in a biblical way so that I am able to serve Christ fully rather than being a slave to bitterness, anger, or fear? Only if I do so can I be free to be the channel of God's blessing to my children."

- "Am I actively training up my children in the way that the Bible says they should go or am I allowing secular educators and morally depraved entertainers to raise them?"

- "Are His Words truly 'on my heart'? Have I bound them as a 'sign on my hand' and as 'frontals on my forehead' (Deuteronomy 6:6-8)? Am I totally committed to what the Bible says on every subject? Do I know the difference between biblical parenting and the failed ideas and philosophies of modern, humanistic parenting? Am I willing to follow the Bible's way even if others criticize me?"

If we can answer yes to the above questions, then we can claim the wonderful, biblical promises of the covenant for our children, that they "shall not depart" from the right and true way and they will experience God's presence and blessings all the days of their lives. If we cannot answer yes to these questions, then we cannot claim these promises. After nearly thirty years of working with children, youth, and their families, I can testify unreservedly that this is true. Some children pay a very heavy price for their parents getting this wrong. Other children grow up and bless their parents for the blessings they experience because of their parent's faithfulness.

But it's not just the children who are blessed when parents

fulfill the two covenant priorities of Deuteronomy 6:4-7. The parents receive great blessing as well.

In Genesis chapter 18 God explains one important reason why He chose Abraham out of all the people of the earth and what His purpose was in selecting him.

For I have chosen him, so that he may command ["train up"] his children and his household after him to keep the way of the Lord by doing righteousness and justice, so that the Lord may bring upon Abraham what He has spoken about him.

Genesis 18:19

When we read the words "in order that" twice in the above verse, we see that God is showing us His purpose in establishing His covenant with Abraham and all others who have entered into covenant with God since then. God chose Abraham and taught him His covenant stipulations *so that* he would teach them to his children. Abraham was to "train up" his children in this covenant *so that* all God's promises could come to Abraham.

In other words, one reason that God chose Abraham was that, unlike many parents, he would "train up his children in the way they should go." Then and only then could all the promises God made to Abraham come to pass. Remember, God promised Abraham land, dominion, and, best of all, that all the families of the earth would be blessed in him (Genesis 12:1-3). Although Abraham enjoyed God's presence and blessing throughout his life, many of the promises made to him were fulfilled in his descendants. Only by training his children could these future blessings be secured.

God never changes in His purposes or principles. He still works this way today. A family or a church only secures future blessings by training up their children in God's covenant. So many of the rich blessings that God would bring into our lives will come through our children and grandchildren, but only if we train them up in "the way [they] should go." My greatest prospects for future happiness lie in investing myself to raise up godly children. Failure to do so will bring pain.

Let me cite just one of the many hundreds of examples I could offer. I want to contrast two different families I know. Both brought their families to church each Sunday. Both of the churches they attended were good, evangelical churches. One family had four boys. Now those boys are grown, and not one is involved in church. Among them there is a history of alcohol and drug abuse, pregnant girlfriends, abortions, broken relationships, and even scrapes with the law.

The second family had seven children. All seven are married and active in their churches. Two are ministers and one is a principal of a Christian school. None have been involved in drugs and alcohol, and there are many wonderful grandchildren.

Was God unfair to the one family? Certainly not; God's promise was offered to both. However, the promise comes with two conditions, neither of which is satisfied by merely sitting through a church service with your kids. Only one family met the conditions. The parents of the one family loved God with all their hearts. They did not give God a secondary place while they pursued lesser things with greater energy. They also trained up their children, taking care of what they were exposed to and learned. They did not turn over the raising of their children to ungodly people. Now in the later years they are experiencing the blessings that God wants to bring into all our lives. The other family is not experiencing these joys because they did not fulfill their part of the covenant.

46

4: The Divine Priority

A Church's Responsibility

In the same way, every church must ask itself how it measures up to the two covenant stipulations of Deuteronomy 6:4-7. Along with teaching their people to love God with all their heart, is reaching and training up their children their top priority? Unless we fulfill this covenant priority, we cannot gain the dominion that God wants to give His church and fulfill its purpose and destiny.

In order to understand our purpose and destiny, we must go to the very beginning. When God created us in His image, He declared His purpose in doing so.

And God said, "Let Us make man in Our image, after Our likeness: and let them have dominion." ["let them rule over," NASB]

Genesis 1:26, KJV

God's purpose in making us in His image was that we might rule and have dominion on earth under Him. Evil and rebellion were already present through Satan. We were to extend God's righteousness and goodness on earth. The fall of man into sin disrupted that assignment. However, this assignment or purpose remains for all who are being restored into Christ's image. The church's purpose is to extend Christ's Kingdom and rule and have dominion under Him.

Now, in order to have dominion we must understand the process by which we are to gain and exercise dominion. God Himself explains the process to us just two verses after creating us to have dominion.

God blessed them; and God said to them, "Be fruitful and multiply, and fill the earth, and subdue it; and rule...."

Genesis 1:28

Before they could rule, they had to subdue the earth. But the precondition to subduing the earth was that they had to "be fruitful and multiply and fill the earth." The first step to dominion is to be fruitful and multiply (that is, have children). God's plan for His people to gain dominion is that they should multiply (children), and then they must train them up in the Word of God.

When Christians begin to value possessions and leisure time more than having children, they begin to surrender dominion. When they fail to fully train their children up in God's covenant ways, then they surrender further dominion. The story of America's decline spiritually and morally over the past thirty-five or forty years is largely a tale of Christians' choosing to have fewer kids and allow secular humanists to train up the children they do have. As a result, the Christian church has forfeited much of its dominion over American culture.

Raising up godly, faithful offspring is the fundamental stewardship and ministry of the people of God. If we fail to do this, we will find that rather than ruling, we will be ruled over. This is a fundamental reality of life that can't be denied.

European civilization, despite its technological and financial superiority, is rapidly being eclipsed because of the failure of Europeans to have children. Their nations are being surrendered to other non-Christian, non-democratic cultures. They are in real danger of losing their way of life. Unless you have children and are able to pass on to them your faith and values, you will decline.

As important as evangelism is, it can't substitute for the covenant responsibility to bring up children "in the discipline and instruction of the Lord" (Ephesians 6:4). A church that is built primarily of converts can never be as strong and stable as a church that is built upon people who were brought up in God's covenant. If we

48

are to win our culture and our world, we must increase both through evangelism and growth of Christian families.

We must all ask ourselves if our church is fulfilling this covenant requirement.

- Are we bucking current cultural trends and actively encouraging Christian couples to have larger families?

- Are we highlighting and celebrating the blessings and joys of having children? Our culture teaches that children are economic liabilities (robbing us of gaining possessions) and an intrusion upon plans for self-fulfillment. For this reason many Christian couples are choosing to have not more than two children. God, however, has a different view.

Behold, children are a gift of the Lord, the fruit of the womb is a reward. Like arrows in the hand of a warrior, so are the children of one's youth. How blessed is the man whose quiver is full.

Psalm 127:3-5

- Are we supporting parents in their ministry to their children by offering them parent training and mentoring and educational options for their kids? Does our church offer scholarship help to parents who want their kids to have a Christian education? If we say that we can't afford it, then maybe we need to rethink our priorities.

- When it comes to ministering to the kids God brings to our church, have we truly made it a top priority?

  - Is it reflected in our budget?

  - Do we have some of our very best people working on it?

- Do we honor our volunteers in this area, making them feel like their work is vitally important?

- Is it reflected in salary and staffing decisions?

- Do we provide mentors, activities, programs, and camps that successfully connect with our young and bring lasting transformation?

We must do more than just give lip service. We must make a searching inventory. For instance, at our church the youth pastor and children's pastor earn the same income as every other associate pastor and have the same benefits package. This explains why they have both remained in those positions for more than fifteen years. In addition, our various ministries related to children and youth traditionally take up the largest part of our budget each year. This should not be exceptional but rather the norm at most churches across our nation.

This is God's pattern, and we will not succeed if we ignore it. In order to be truly blessed we must return to the simple covenant requirements of Deuteronomy 6.

The future prospects of our families, churches, and nation depend upon the investment we make in our children today. What kind of a nation and church will we experience in our future years? We will determine that today? What kind of families will surround us in our later years? Will our declining years be blessed or troubled? We will determine the answers to those questions today. It all depends upon whether we will "love the Lord our God with all our heart, with all our might and with all our soul" and whether we will "train up our children in the way they should go."

5

For Richie and Andy

Richie was a senior at a high school near our church that many of our young people attend. He was a week away from graduating, according to a newspaper report. Late on a Monday afternoon, January 19, he put aside an art project he had been working on and wrote a note to his parents which he left on the dining room table. He got up and left the house without saying a word. He walked two miles to Wal-Mart carrying a can of paint thinner. He cut across the parking lot and scrambled down the bank to the dry San Diego River bed. He poured the paint thinner over his head and body, flicked his lighter and then set himself on fire. Eleven hours later he was pronounced dead at the U.C.S.D. Burn Center.

The *San Diego Union*, which carried the story, struggled to understand why Richie would do such a thing. They included the lyrics to one of the songs that Richie had written for his band:

Life sucks then you die, you might as well end it now.
Graduate, be all you can be, yeah, right, I disagree.
You've got courage I can see to live through this misery.
Life sucks, then you die, you've got no future anyway.[8]

While very few of our young people do anything as dramatic and sudden as Richie's suicide, many do share Richie's philosophy and live aimless and self-destructive lives. The problem is not that

---

[8] Caitlin Rother, "A Painful End," *Union Tribune* [San Diego], 15 Mar. 1998.

they are poor students or slow learners. The problem is that they have learned the lessons they have been taught *too well.* Our schools and popular media give them no absolutes or purpose for their life, and in many cases neither can their parents. Consequently, many children today grow up in a moral and spiritual vacuum with little or no direction given to them. *The result is confusion, apathy, lack of self-control, anger, and despair.*

This is because we are spiritual beings created in the image of God who created us to live in relationship and service to Him. This is what gives our lives purpose and worth. Deprived of this knowledge, many young people begin to spiral into aimlessness and destruction.

What so many kids desperately need are adults who can give them support, direction, spiritual instruction, and accountability. God's plan is that parents should be the primary ones to fill that role. Many parents, however, are failing to do this. Because of out-of-wedlock births, divorces, and death, many parents, especially fathers, are not physically available to the child. In addition, many custodial parents are emotionally unavailable because they are consumed by their own struggles with drug and alcohol addiction, broken relationships, or some other personal agenda. The result is many kids who feel alienated and alone.

Several years earlier Richie had written these words in a school essay.

Nobody's ever looked inside and seen my crying tears.
I'm grungy on the outside, not respectable at all.
I am myself and I'll always be, until the day I fall.
Because no one really feels my thoughts, and no one really cares.[9]

---

⁹Rother, "A Painful End."

5: For Richie and Andy

Tens of thousands of kids in every city feel lost and alone. They attempt to distract themselves with amusements, losing themselves for hours in video games or online activities. Others lose themselves in a frantic schedule of outward busyness while inwardly they feel empty. Still others attempt to numb their inner pain with drugs and alcohol.

These kids are a generation crying out for attention and direction. Through Youth Venture[10] and our other various outreaches we have met them by the thousands, and they are spiritually hungry. In fact, in a recent survey,[11] six in ten teens reported that "being close to God" was important to them. We witness this every day as we watch how teens respond to our Youth Venture mentoring lessons. They are hungry for spiritual answers. And too often no one is supplying them with these answers.

The crisis among our youth is well known and has been with us for some time. In the thirty years following the Supreme Court's removal of Bible reading (1962) and prayer (1963) from our public schools the unwed pregnancy rate increased by nearly 600 percent,[12] the suicide rate among teenagers rose by 300 percent[13] as did the rate for juvenile violent crimes.[14] Student SAT scores dropped nearly 10 percent during that same period even though spending for education increased.[15] Our national leaders had taken something very precious from America's youth, and into that vacuum came demons of confusion and destruction. Drug and alcohol abuse as well as gangs have become epidemic. The plight of young people today is serious.

---

[10]Youth Venture is a series of four neighborhood youth centers that our church operates in our community which features mentoring programs, camps, and various activities.

[11]Barna 80.

[12]National Center for Health Statistics, Table 1-1. Live Births, Birth Rates, and Fertility Rates, by Race: United States, 1901-2000 http://www.cdc.gov/nchs/data/statab/t001x01.pdf (May 15, 2007).

[13]http://www.cdc.gov/nchs/data/statab/t001x01.pdf.

[14]FBI, as sited in William J. Bennett, *The Index of Leading Cultural Indicators: American Society at the End of the Twentieth Century*, (New York: Broadway Books, 1999) 21-22.

[15]The College Board and US Dept of Ed as cited in William J. Bennett, *The Index of Leading Cultural Indicators: Facts and Figures on the State of American Society*, (New York: Simon & Schuster Inc., 1994) 82-84.

The Joshua Principle

The status quo is, or should be, completely unacceptable to us, yet year after year passes with no substantive changes taking place. We seem to be more willing to accept the terrible carnage among our youth than to do things differently. This was poignantly illustrated in our town. Just several years after Richie's tragic death, an even greater tragedy took place at his former school that made international headlines.

Andy Williams was a small, skinny, baby-faced fifteen-year-old freshman. According to newspaper reports, his parents had divorced when he was three and he had just moved into the area a year and a half before with his father. Because of his small size and small town background, he was mercilessly bullied by the neighborhood kids he hung out with. He grew deeply depressed and began smoking marijuana every day.

According to those same accounts, one morning he got up and broke into his father's gun cabinet and removed a 22-caliber hand-gun and 40 rounds of ammunition. He packed it in his school backpack along with a toy monkey named Spunkey, which he had been given as a gift when he was nine years old. He put on his backpack and headed off to school. At 9:20 a.m. he entered one of the bathrooms at school and loaded the revolver in a bathroom stall. As he emerged he began firing. He shot two students in the bathroom, one fatally. Then he left the bathroom and opened fire on the students in the courtyard. When it was over, two students were dead and thirteen others wounded, including two adults.[1]

Andy was a dramatic illustration of the toxic culture that our kids are growing up in and the complete failure of our publicly funded institutions to deal with these problems. And yet year after year few real changes are made. People who look to the government or our schools to solve the problems of our youth are

---

[1] ABC News, *Exclusive: Santana School Shooter*, October 10, 2001. https://abcnews.go.com/Primetime/story?id=132072&page=1

living in denial. *Apparently, continuing to push a failed secular, humanistic agenda is more important than the lives of our nation's youth.*

Hope for our nations children lies in only two places: the family and the church.

Jamming the Machine

Presently in America there is a great machine that grinds up and destroys our young. It's everywhere, even reaching into the womb. Even there our children are not safe. A multi-billion dollar abortion industry has destroyed more than a quarter of the children who were conceived over the past thirty-five years. If they survive the womb, the machine is waiting there for them on the day of their birth. It seeks to harm them through an epidemic of physical and sexual abuse. It wounds their soul through a culture of easy, no-fault divorce and broken homes. It continues its assault on their hearts and minds with a humanistic, secular education, a morally depraved entertainment industry, a dangerous and predatory internet culture, the availability of drugs and alcohol, and a culture of moral confusion and sexual license. Together it forms a great machine that grinds up and destroys the spiritual, moral, and physical lives of our kids. Relatively few kids survive it without serious problems.

Little help will come from government social programs or our education system. They are often a part of the problem. The only answer is for people who are touched by the love of God to place their lives into the gears of this machine and stop it long enough to pull a child out. It will require people who are willing to win the war for our children one child at a time.

God has always called His people to a special concern for the young. It's an essential part of authentic faith.

Pure and undefiled religion in the sight of our God and Father is this: to visit orphans and widows in their distress, and to keep oneself unstained by the world.
James 1:27, emphasis mine

Today our society has created a new class of orphans. They are orphaned spiritually and often emotionally and they are in dire need of our love and attention. God has always called his faithful followers to protect and care for them.

Learn to do good; seek justice, reprove the ruthless, defend the orphan, plead for the widow.
Isaiah 1:17, emphasis mine

Vindicate the weak and fatherless; do justice to the afflicted and destitute. Rescue the weak and needy; deliver them out of the hand of the wicked.
Psalm 82:3-4, emphasis mine

It's too late for Richie and Andy, but it's not too late for millions of others if only we will obey God's call. I have often wondered how different things might have been for Richie and especially for Andy (and all those whose lives they affected) if only one of our Youth Venture Teen Centers had been in their neighborhoods.

I'm glad to say that we now have a Youth Venture Teen Center in Santee and are looking for the Richies and Andys that are all around us. We have seen many lives changed through the love of people at our Youth Ventures. One such youngster was Tavis. Here is his story in his own words.

Tavis' Story

"My home life growing up was horrible. I was born into a family of partiers who thought of nothing except the next high. If I was hungry, I had to fend for myself. If I had clothes to wear, it was because a friend gave me hand-me-downs. No one at home cared for me and, honestly, I don't think they loved me either.

"At a young age I was filled with anger and became violent. I wanted to fight pretty much everyone I came in contact with and was suspended from school several times. Eventually my violent behavior got me kicked out of junior high school.

"I had a friend named Jason who had a terrible home life just like me. He was violent, like me, and even though we started out as enemies, we quickly became friends.

"When I was in seventh or eighth grade, I really wanted to fight a kid named Dustin. There was no particular reason, but something inside of me told me to follow him after school and fight him. Dustin hung out a Youth Venture Teen Center, an after-school game room run by the church he attended.

"Jason and I followed Dustin to Youth Venture, but before I could fight him, I was intercepted by Pastor Mark Hoffman, the founder of Youth Venture. He knew I was there to fight, so he pulled me aside and told me I'd have to leave if I insisted on making trouble. Then he did something that I thought was completely crazy. He asked if he could pray for me. What a weird thing to ask me! Still, something made me agree to have him pray for me.

"He never laid a hand on me, but when he began to pray I felt like something hit me that was overwhelming. It felt powerful and loving all at the same time. It was the strangest thing I had ever experienced. I learned later that it was the Holy Spirit.

"I was a tough guy and didn't want to admit it, but his prayer had gone deep inside me and touched my heart. I thought, 'I came down here to start a fight, but instead of throwing me out like everyone else in my life has done, he wanted to help me.' I wanted to know more about what had happened to me during that prayer, so I started going to Youth Venture regularly after school.

"People there began to accept me and love me. I never had that at home, and soon Youth Venture became my second home—and certainly the home I preferred. The counselors and volunteers really took care of me. I had a mentor who often bought me something to eat when I showed up. There were many times that the meal he bought me was the only one I had eaten that day. I always left Youth Venture with a smile even though things would be horrible when I got home. I held on because I knew I could go back to Youth Venture the next day and everything would be all right.

"Through Youth Venture I met people who loved me and prayed for me. I had a powerful encounter during a youth camp they invited me to attend. God was showing me how much He loved me and what a great price He had paid to rescue me. It was awesome.

"Today I have a beautiful wife and a high-paying job working in security and management for a multimillion-dollar property. My life is so different than it started out.

"I see clearly how my life could have turned out if I had taken the other path. All I have to do is look at Jason. He refused to accept Pastor Hoffman's help. Jason saw himself as a tough guy who didn't need anyone. While I was going to Youth Venture, Jason continued down that violent road. Today Jason is serving a life sentence in prison for murder.

"I am so thankful to God that He intercepted me before I had gone too far down that dark road."

6

Hidden Treasure

A gem dealer was strolling down the aisles at a mineral show when he noticed a blue-violet stone the size of a potato. He looked it over, then as calmly as possible asked the vendor, "You want $15 for this?" The seller, realizing the rock wasn't as pretty as others in the bin, lowered the price to $10. The stone has since been certified as a 1,905-carat natural star sapphire, about 800 carats larger than the next largest stone of its kind. It was appraised at $2.28 million.[2] It took someone who knew and loved stones to realize its true worth.

God sees great value where others do not. God's value system is so different from that of so many Christians. When many Christians go to the malls to shop, their eyes are on the shiny treasures behind the store windows. They dream and plan how they can make those treasures theirs, but they miss the true treasures. They walk right past the kids who aimlessly hang out at the mall entrances and food courts. In fact, they *hurry* past these unruly young people who bum cigarettes and sometimes sex from each other. After all, with their lack of manners, baggy clothes and dyed hair they seem foreign and unappealing.

We miss their value and potential because of the condition in which we find them. They are like that natural star sapphire in the story above. Before it was cut and polished it looked like a

[2] United Press International, *World's Largest Star Sapphire Found at Show: Rocks to Riches: $10 Stone Worth $2.28 Million, Los Angeles Times*, November 12, 1986.

valueless rock, but the true value of something is established by what someone is willing to pay for it.

The greatest price ever paid was that of the blood of the only Son of God. And only one thing in this world could command such a price. It's the human soul. The souls of many of our young people who hang out at malls, ride their skateboards at parks, and surf the net are crying out for those who will recognize their worth and be willing to pay the price to reach them.

Things of great worth are always costly. The greatest achievements always require the greatest effort and sacrifice. So it is with souls. They can't be won by those who fail to recognize their true worth. Such people are unwilling to pay the necessary price or make the required sacrifice, but those who *are* willing win these treasures for their Master.

Whenever I see a young person acting foolishly, whenever I observe a group of youths doing destructive acts, I always ask myself, *"How would I be acting if I had only been taught what they have been taught and only knew what they know? How might I look? What might my values be?"*

The Power of Influence

The older and wiser I become, the more I am thankful for the influence of my parents and the other adults who shaped me as I grew up. I am thankful for the Christian education I received up through eighth grade. Certainly, had it not been for their influence, my life would have turned out very differently. I am keenly aware of the power of influence in shaping a life.

Imagine you are holding in your hand a simple bar of steel, the kind of rolled steel used to manufacture things. It would cost 15 to

20 dollars. Now, if you took that bar of steel and manufactured it into two horseshoes, it would be worth 35 to 40 dollars. However, if you took that same bar of steel and made it into sewing needles, its value would be 400 dollars. But, believe it or not, if you took that same steel and created the very precise gears that go into a very fine watch, its value would be 250,000 dollars.

Like that rolled steel, a child's or youth's life is raw material. Their value will be determined by what kind of person they become. That in large part will depend upon what people and forces influence them. And that, my friend, is up to us. Are we in the church willing to be the shaping influence? To make a lasting and significant impression in someone's life is not cheap or easy. Often it takes years. The cost and effort required are great because the potential is so great.

An old parable says that a group of tourists were touring a German village that had been there for centuries. They came upon an old man sitting on his porch. One of the tourists asked him, "Were there any great men born in this village?" The wise old man answered him, "No, only babies."

Greatness or character is not guaranteed by genes. No one is born great, nor is character or greatness denied because of genes. Everyone is born with the potential of great character and achievement. It's largely dependent upon what others invest in them and what they then do with what they are given.

What will the church of tomorrow be like? What will America be like in twenty, thirty, or forty years? The answer is not in the genes. The answer lies with you and me, fellow Christian. It depends upon what we decide to invest in young people.

Buying the Field

Jesus told a parable about a treasure which a man found hidden in a field. He said that in order to gain the treasure, the man had to sell all his possessions to first buy the field, and only then could the treasure be his (Matthew 13:44). The treasure was a fabulous one. But only the one who bought the field could rightfully claim the treasure, and the price of the field was great.

The treasure we seek is human souls, and along with that a better future for everyone. This treasure is often hidden in a field (Matthew 13:44). Jesus taught us that to gain the treasure we must be willing to buy the field. That field is the world of children and youth. Unless we can approach and enter that world and pay the price required, we cannot claim the treasure.

One treasure we found in the field was a boy named Kyle.

Kyle's Story

"When I was growing up, we moved many times. Sometimes we would move every few months. Once we lived in our car and in motels for a year and a half. My dad sold drugs out of our home. When he wasn't on drugs, he was sleeping. My mom worked, but she also did drugs. Mostly they did crystal meth. I remember a drug dealer coming over and beating my dad up right in front of me on our porch. There was blood all over the door.

"There were always people over at my house doing drugs, so I tried to be gone as much as possible. There was seldom any food at my house, and I was embarrassed at school because I had to wear the same dirty clothes day after day. I used to steal everything I needed from the mall. I was full of anger. It's how I dealt with my problems.

"One day my friend John and I were walking across the 7-11 parking lot looking for cigarette butts on the ground to smoke. We looked up and saw this building with the words 'Youth Venture.' We looked inside and saw that there were free games. We went again the next day and got invited to go on a trip to the beach. I hardly ever got to go to the beach, so I jumped at the chance.

"I began to get more involved. A man named Henry began to hang out with me and mentor me. He would buy me food and take me through the Youth Venture mentoring lessons. I began to learn about God and His plans for me. It was all new. There was never a Bible in my house, and I don't ever remember being inside a church growing up.

"Youth Venture became my home. I felt loved and safe there. One day Pastor Mark invited me to go to a camp they were holding. He said I could go for free because some businessman would pay for me. Camp was the best week of my life.

"At camp God began to open up my heart. He showed me that these were people who really cared for me and would stick by me. For the first time in my life I realized that there were people I could trust.

"At the evening meeting of the last night of camp, I had an experience with God that changed my life. As the others began to sing worship songs to God, I closed my eyes and tried to picture what God would be like. As I concentrated on God, all of my rage and anger seemed to leave me. I remembered that someone at Youth Venture had told me that Jesus loved me so much that He had died on a cross for me. I wanted to know this Jesus and His love.

"Immediately His love seemed to fall upon me and fill me to overflowing. Now I knew that it was all real. The anger and hatred just left, replaced by His perfect love. I was born again. I felt like I was going to explode with joy and relief.

"Gradually, but surely, my life changed. I continued to hang out at Youth Venture. I became a leader that people looked up to. As I got older I started to help out with the kids' ministry at church. I graduated from high school this year, and I am thankful for all the people from Youth Venture who opened up their hearts and homes to me. I'm attending college now and want to become a children's church pastor because I know firsthand the difference God can make in a life."

Gaining the Treasure

In Proverbs 13:22 we read that "The wealth of the sinner is stored up for the righteous." God wants to give the wealth of the unrighteous to godly people who are His stewards. Think about it. The greatest wealth or treasure the unrighteous have is their children. God is seeking to give the church the world's children as our inheritance. He wants to give us a harvest of souls greater than we have dared to think.

Are you willing to enter the world of children and youth with all its confusion, pain and sin? Will you buy the field? Will you claim the treasure?

7

Understanding Youth

One of the great challenges in ministering to adolescents and teens is in understanding them. The truth is that most people are uncomfortable being around teenagers. Adolescence is a unique stage of development that is different from both childhood and adulthood. Adolescents see and experience life differently than adults. It's one reason why both they and their parents often feel misunderstood by each other.

In order to be an effective minister to them, we must understand their world. That is, we must understand the way that they see and experience the world. In order to do this we must understand adolescence from two different perspectives.

God's Design

First, we must see *adolescence from the perspective of our Creator's intent.* Remember that adolescence is God's invention. It's part of His design to produce mature sons and daughters who can love and serve Him. We must be able to rejoice in it as an exciting, God-given stage of development in our Creator's wise and good plan. Later in the book we'll consider adolescence from the perspective of a societal creation.

Adolescence is the stage of development that transitions a human being from childhood to adulthood. Unlike the earlier stages that marked childhood, like infancy, toddler, preschool, and grade school, the key word for adolescence is not *development* but rather *change*. No longer is the child merely growing into the next stage of childhood, but he is now changing into an adult.

- Physically their bodies are changing to be able to do adult work and, even more importantly, to have the power to reproduce.

- Mentally they are undergoing a profound change. They are moving from childhood's concrete reasoning to the adult ability to do abstract reasoning. Just like the physical changes in the body produce awkwardness and a lack of coordination during adolescence, so these changes produce absentmindedness and forgetfulness.

- Emotionally they are changing to the greater emotional abilities and capacities of adults. These changes will give them the emotional resources and strength to maintain a lifelong marriage covenant, display the sacrificial love necessary to be parents, and survive the demands of the world outside of the family. Like the physical and mental stages, there is awkwardness as well as the adolescent tries to understand and master these emerging emotional capabilities. Adolescents display moodiness and emotional swings. Their "highs" are very high and their "lows" are very low. They easily become giddy and silly and they also cry easily. They are sometimes perplexed, knowing that they are not in control of their emotions

- Spiritually they are changing to become people who have their own faith. Children believe whatever their parents believe. Their faith is largely a reflection of their parents' faith. The changes taking place during adolescence, however, bring about the opportunity for them to develop a deep faith held by their own personal conviction. Adolescence, therefore, includes a crisis of faith. The opportunity to choose must, by definition, include the opportunity to refuse. *It's for this reason that adolescence, especially early adolescence (ages ten to fourteen), must be the focus of the church's greatest efforts and energies.*

- Socially they are developing the ability to separate from their family so that they can go out and form their own families. Psychologists refer to this process as "individuation," and, like other facts of adolescent change, they can be quite clumsy at this as well. This is referred to in Genesis, where we read:

*For this cause a man shall **leave** his father and his mother, and shall **cleave** to his wife; and they shall become one flesh.*
Genesis 2:24, NASB 77,
emphasis mine

Unless one successfully leaves (individuates) from one's *family of origin,* they can never fully cleave (become one) with their new spouse and form a new family. It's necessary that this process be completed successfully if the adolescent is ever going to be able to go on and have a successful, healthy family of his or her own.

While individuation is both good and necessary, rebellion is neither good nor necessary. Contrary to what many people seem to think, individuation is indeed a phase that all kids have to go through, but rebelliousness is not. *Rebelliousness is not a necessary part of the process God designed. Rather, rebelliousness is a result of a breakdown in the individuation process.* In healthy families, individuation is a goal shared by both the adolescent and the parent. Both desire growing independence for the child. Healthy parents merely want to ensure that such growing independence is matched with a growing display of responsibility. It's probably unavoidable that parents and adolescence will not always agree at exactly how fast freedoms should be granted. The Bible, however, gives authoritative and objective guidance. If both the parents and the adolescent follow the instructions in God's Word, then rebellion (with all the pain and destruction it brings) can be avoided.

Although God loves children, He does not want them to remain children forever. His purpose in giving us children is that He might raise up *productive adult sons and daughters* who can fully function as His partners in the mission of His Kingdom. He wants men and women who can reproduce physically and spiritually, who can guide, guard and govern, and who produce more than they consume. He wants sons and daughters who can triumph over Satan and have dominion in their own lives, marriages, families, and society. Adolescence is the period in which children are meant to change into such adults. Since adolescence is such a critical and defining period in God's plan, it's not surprising that this challenging time has become such a battleground. This brings us to the second dimension of adolescence.

Youth Culture

The second perspective from which we must be able to view adolescence is *adolescence as a social creation.* By this I am referring to many aspects of the "youth culture" that have proven to be a dangerous and very costly diversion from the road to adulthood. Many such things as fashions, music, fads, and various behaviors such as drug use, gangs, and alcohol have fueled rebellion and caused a rupture between the generations. As stated above, rebellion is not a necessary part of adolescence. Of my three sons, the third one is going through the teen years, but none of them have rebelled. Their teen years have been some of the best times we've had together. Rebellion is an avoidable breakdown in the growing-up process between parents and children and is further fueled by outside sources. By wisely monitoring and limiting the access these forces have to our kids, we can help save our kids from the confusion and rebelliousness of so many of their peers.

Many of these forces are in play because adult businessmen have figured out that there are billions of dollars to be made in exploiting the naiveté, confusion, awkwardness, and pain of young people. Whether you are talking about pornography, drugs, alcohol, cigarettes, or violent rap music, these are all problems that adults are causing for kids. After all, it's adults who produce and smuggle drugs, who produce and market alcohol and cigarettes, who design and produce the fashions kids wear, and who produce the movies kids watch and the music they listen to. Huge industries and billions of dollars depend upon inciting rebellion and widening the gap between the generations.

Discerning the Difference

In order to minister to young people, we must be able to discern in their behavior what we are dealing with. Is the particular behavior we are observing merely a result of the awkwardness and absent-mindedness caused by all the changes taking place in them during the adolescent process or is that behavior really rebellion? Do we need to exercise love and patience or stern discipline? A lot rides on getting it right.

Often older children and teens are criticized and scolded, and thereby alienated from church, for being nothing more than what God has made them. Many churches have driven away their youth because they refuse to accept the noise, agitation, and broken

69

furniture that seems to be an inseparable part of having children and adolescents around. These churches have all entered into a death process. Many of them have already died and shut their doors. Other churches, understanding God's plan and purpose, have valued youth. They have refused to make their personal preferences and tastes absolute. They have been willing to make adjustments to their comfort zone and accommodations to their preferences in order to make youth feel welcomed and loved. These churches are blessed and continue to be renewed and experience growth.

I have observed that much of the conflict between adolescents and their parents and other adults comes from a lack of understanding of what is normal during adolescence. But how can we tell what part of their behavior is normal and what part is rebellion? That is, what part of it is a result of sin and self-centeredness and what part of it is merely the unavoidable result of the process that God has them going through? It can be difficult at times to tell the difference. Many parents excuse and ignore blatant rebellion and dangerous behavior by saying, "It's just a phase that they all have to go through." Of course, it's very obvious that it's not just a phase since so many of our teenagers never come out of it. They live much of the rest of their lives in bondage to many of the choices that they made in their adolescent years. In America, adolescence and the teen years have become a dangerous never-never land, a black hole that many young people never fully emerge from, even into their thirty's and forty's.

But how can we know what is normal and acceptable? After all, every adolescent we meet is affected by the fallen sin nature. Their actions are a confusing mixture of what God has programmed in them and the fact that they are fallen, prideful, self-centered beings who are further incited by a youth culture that's hostile and negative. If only there was a sinless boy or girl, one without a fallen

70

nature that could serve as a model or measure of what is normal. If only we could observe him as he went through the adolescent process just the way God designed it, then we would know what is acceptable and normal. Well, God has provided us with a record of just such an adolescent. We will meet him in the next chapter.

The Joshua Principle

8

Learning From Jesus the Adolescent

A s we noted earlier, there is only one story of Jesus between the accounts of His birth and the beginning of His ministry at age thirty. It's the story of Jesus at the temple in Jerusalem at age twelve.

This story is told in the second chapter of the Gospel of Luke. Try to read this account as though for the first time. Read it literally without any filters or preconceptions. What do we learn about adolescence?

The Child continued to grow and become strong, increasing in wisdom; and the grace of God was upon Him. Now His parents went to Jerusalem every year at the Feast of the Passover. And when He became twelve, they went up there according to the custom of the Feast; and as they were returning, after spending the full number of days, the boy Jesus stayed behind in Jerusalem. But His parents were unaware of it, but supposed Him to be in the caravan, and went a day's journey; and they began looking for Him among their relatives and acquaintances. When they did not find Him, they returned to Jerusalem looking for Him. Then, after three days they found Him in the temple, sitting in the midst of the teachers, both listening to them and asking them questions. And all who heard Him were amazed at His understanding and His answers. When they saw Him, they were astonished; and His mother said to Him, "Son, why have You treated us this way? Behold, Your father and I have been anxiously looking for You." And He said to them, "Why is it that you were looking for Me? Did you not know that I had to be in My Father's house?" But they did not understand the statement which He had made to them.

Luke 2:40-50

So What's Normal?

In considering what this teaches us about adolescence, remember that the Bible teaches us that Jesus was without sin. That means that at no point in His life did He ever sin. This is a central tenet of Christianity. It further means that whatever Jesus did in this story, no matter how much it inconvenienced or frustrated His parents, it was not sin, rebellion, or self-centeredness, but simply the result of going through adolescence. Note what we learn from the only human being who ever went through the adolescent process without sin.

In verse 40, we read that Jesus is referred to as a *"child."* This verse is a summary statement of Jesus going through the childhood stage, that is, Jesus is developing gradually or progressively, or as it states: "The child *continued to grow and become strong.*" Verse 43 however marks a clear change. A different word is used to describe Jesus. Here Jesus is referred to as a *"boy."* The word "child" is genderless; however, the word "boy" speaks of a clear sexual identity. This signals that Jesus has already left the stage of childhood and entered adolescence where sexual identity is really developed. Everything is changing. Jesus has entered the mysterious world of adolescence.

Individuation

In verses 42-44 we see the *process* of individuation taking places in Jesus' life. Jesus' parents took Him to the feast with them. Jesus was not yet an adult, and they were continuing to guide His spiritual development and set the boundaries of His life. At the same time they are gradually giving Him greater freedom within those boundaries. He is allowed to separate and move with some freedom while in Jerusalem, something He would not have been allowed as a child. In other words, Jesus' parents are managing the process. This is, of course, where parents must pray for God's wisdom and follow the directions in His Word.

Verses 43-50 give us a window into adolescent development.

Inquisitiveness

We see in verse 46 *a new level of inquisitiveness in Jesus.* We see Him sitting in the midst of the teachers of the Law asking questions. The reason I say that this is a new development is because it's the last place his parents look for Him, not the first. It's only after several days that they think to look among the teachers at the temple. If that had been His habit in previous years, it would have been the first place that they would have looked. Jesus at age nine or ten was not able or motivated to ask those questions, but now He has an insatiable desire to question and know the reasons for what He has been taught. Adolescence is a time of searching and inquisitiveness. New intellectual abilities for abstract reasoning cause them to search out the truth of what they have been taught. As children, they accepted it simply because their parents said it. Now the time has come for them to live from personal conviction, being fully convinced themselves.

75

This means that they will question everything and ask hard questions. They will even question core beliefs. This is not necessarily rebellion but part of their God-given assignment. The real problem comes when the church or parents are not available or prepared to answer their questions and others are standing by who are ready to supply the wrong answers. Once someone accepts the wrong answers at this pivotal age, it will be very difficult to change their thinking.

New Level of Spiritual Capacity

In the story, *Jesus has entered a new stage* where He can have His own separate identity in God and His own sense of call. As a child, Jesus *accompanied* His parents to religious observances, but now He is fully able to have *His own* spiritual convictions. He says in verse 49, "Did you not know that I had to be in My Father's house?" This statement reveals that Jesus has a deep sense of His own personal call from God. This becomes possible during adolescence.

It's obvious that we are seeing *a new level of spiritual interest and capacity in Jesus.* Verse 47 tells us that the teachers were amazed at Jesus' understanding. When Joseph and Mary arrived they did not say, "Oh well, that's just the way He is. He has always demonstrated this deep spirituality. We are so proud of Him." Rather we read in verse 48 that when they found Jesus and observed what was happening, "They were astonished." They were unaware that Jesus had such a deep spiritual hunger and capacity. The reason is familiar to most parents. Our kids grow up so fast that we often can't keep up with them. Jesus had developed a spiritual capacity far beyond what his parents had realized. Probably they had been too busy with the demands of everyday life to notice His growth.

Some things never change. It's usually very amusing to watch the reactions of parents when you compliment them on the spiritual depth and maturity their child demonstrated at camp or youth group. You are usually greeted with a "deer caught in the headlights" stare that says, "Are you sure you know who you are talking to? I think you have me mixed up with the parents of some other kid." I have on many occasions actually had parents say those very words to me in all sincerity. They are not aware of how their child's spiritual capabilities are changing. Many Christian parents consistently underestimate the spiritual development of their children. One major reason is given to us in verse 48. It's part of the puzzle of adolescent development.

After being astonished at this display of His piety and godliness they ask the obvious question, "Son, why have You treated us this way? Behold, Your father and I have been anxiously looking for You." What a paradox. Jesus displays such spiritual depth and godliness before the religious leaders and yet is so *seemingly* thoughtless and disrespectful toward His parents. Was Jesus just being an insincere hypocrite? Of course we know that Jesus was not being intentionally thoughtless, disrespectful, or hypocritical. We know this because all of those behaviors are sin, and Jesus never sinned. *There must be another explanation.*

Absentmindedness

Think of all that Jesus' parents were put through. Think of their great inconvenience. Think how much they must have worried. After all, Jerusalem was a city of tens of thousands of people. No doubt they were tempted to wring Jesus' neck. And yet, through all of that, Jesus didn't sin. He was merely being an adolescent. *Jesus was so engrossed in His world of exploration that He had absentmindedly lost track of the time* several days earlier when the caravan He was supposed to have been a part of left Jerusalem. Now, let's admit, that's a pretty big thing to miss. I know it's hard to imagine, and I don't want to be disrespectful here, but Jesus was acting like any other airhead adolescent.

Who can be as absentminded as an adolescent? I remember telling my own kids a thousand times to do something. They would answer with something like, "As soon as I finish this problem," or, "Okay, Dad, I'll do it at the next commercial," or, "As soon as I get home." Well, you know the rest of it. An hour later it still isn't done. When I reminded them, they would get up immediately and do it. It wasn't that they were being intentionally disobedient. They honestly forgot. They could forget anything in the time it took to walk from the living room to the kitchen. The adolescent process is taxing mental work and often they are on overload. There is simply too much happening for them to be able to concentrate on everything. Little things, you know like missing a camel caravan departure, just fall through the cracks. This helps explain the great paradox that we see in our adolescents.

At one point they can seem so godly and the next they can seem self-absorbed and thoughtless of others. Certainly this puzzled and troubled Jesus' parents. But it's not necessarily sinful, as we saw in the case of Jesus. *Now be honest, what would be your first knee-jerk reaction if your son or daughter or some member of your youth group would have pulled what Jesus did?* What words would come out of your mouth? What actions would you take? What consequences would you put into play? Would you be harsh or understanding? How would the twelve-year-old Jesus have been treated by many churches today for this incident?

Stop and Think

Jesus' parents would have been wrong to speak harshly to Jesus, question His character, or punish Him. They may well have put some constructive disciplines in place to help Jesus learn to prioritize and lessen the chance of missing important deadlines in the future (like homework, reports, tests, or camel caravans). After all, part of the parents' job is to assist their child in becoming an adult. But to punish a child as though the embarrassing pratfalls of adolescence are a moral failing is to further humiliate them and cause them to be embittered toward you. I promise that whether you are a parent or a youth leader, if you punish without understanding, you will cause the youth to lose respect for you and you will breed rebellion. The apostle Paul writes:

> *Fathers, **do not provoke your children to anger**, but bring them up in the discipline and instruction of the Lord.*
>
> Ephesians 6:4, emphasis mine

One way that we provoke anger and rebellion is by punishing them for that which they can't completely control. When we discipline them for the foibles of adolescence, then *we are punishing them for who they are.* They will see this as rejection. They will conclude that we do not like or accept them. They will rebel and attempt to deal with their pain by lashing out at us, the ones who are causing them pain. They will try to avoid us. This is exactly how many teens feel about church. They feel alienated, misunderstood, and unappreciated. Many adults apparently view them as some sort of disease to be quarantined.

There is a certain amount of misunderstanding that is unavoidable between the generations. Adolescents simply are unable to see things or react to things the same as adults. The lens through which they see the world seems as normal to them as the one through which the adult is looking. But each lens puts a different color or perspective on the scene. The lens through which the adolescent is looking may be less mature and therefore less accurate; however, it's the lens they have been given. It's not one they have willfully chosen. It's a result of going through the process of adolescence.

Look at the story of Jesus at the Temple. Both He and His parents were mutually perplexed at each other. They ask Jesus, "Why have you treated us this way?" (Luke 2:48). Jesus, for His part, asks them in essence, *"Why is it you didn't know where to look for Me right away? Don't you understand Me at all?"* (see Luke 2:49). Jesus is perplexed that His parents haven't kept up with the changes and development that are going on within Him. The parents, for their part, are further perplexed, for we read:

> *But they did not understand the statement which He had made to them.*
>
> Luke 2:50

No Volunteers

Please remember that no one volunteers for adolescence. Nobody chooses to go through it. It's a very difficult time. Many people look back at their own adolescence as one of the most difficult and painful times of their life. I know I do.

I remember my own adolescence as an unwelcome change from my happy childhood. I did not invite it into my life. Suddenly, all of my friends seemed to go crazy. Every move, every action I did was scrutinized by my friends and peers. It became obvious that many of my former friends no longer considered me quite as "cool" as before. I was apparently somewhat behind the learning curve of adolescent "cool and acceptable behavior." They would correct the way I looked, stood, spoke, what I wore, and most of all how I acted around girls. There were very rigid rules for everything. In addition to this, my eyesight started to go bad, pimples would sometimes erupt on my face, and I had a hard time controlling my moods, sometimes lashing out at my parents.

People who are going through adolescence deserve our time, patience, and encouragement. It seems that for most adults their adolescence was so painful that they have chosen to wipe the memory of it from their minds. How else can we explain the impatience and critical attitude of so many adults in our churches? Is your church understanding, patient, and supportive of older children and adolescents? Do you make allowances for the fact that adolescents can display apparent thoughtlessness and even carelessness simply because of what they are going through? Or does your church seem to obsess on the messes that adolescents leave behind or the way they seem to forget to put things away or mistreat equipment as though it were a deliberate attack on all that is good and true. In truth, they probably didn't notice the mess, forgot they left anything out, and simply didn't reason out what could happen because of the game they were playing with the microphone, for instance. This would all be a result of the limitations of adolescence.

After all, who among us can't remember from our own adolescence absentmindedly doing something incredibly stupid or destructive? There was that terrible moment when something very valuable broke or some event happened and suddenly you realized for the first time that what you were doing was either very stupid or very dangerous. Do you remember the horrible embarrassment you felt when you realized how dumb what you did would look to others? Let me ask you a question. How did authority figures respond? Were they harsh or understanding? How did they make you feel? How did you feel about them as a result? We must be prepared for a certain level of sloppiness, carelessness, inconsistency, and paradox from our middle school and high school students. We must love and delight in our youth in spite of it all, and we must communicate to them that we delight in them. After all, adolescence is difficult and fraught with dangers exactly because it's so pivotal and decisive a time in one's life. There is no more promising a time to make an investment in a person's life than during adolescence.

Using Wisdom and Discernment

We must ask God for patience and wisdom in dealing with our youth. We can make mistakes in two extremes. One is to punish and devalue youth because they are not like us and we have forgotten what it's like to be like them. This will result in harshness and rejection. The opposite mistake is just as common. Many parents excuse rebellion and ungodly behavior because they believe it's just a phase their children must go through and they are afraid to risk the anger and rejection of their kids by crossing them. The fact is that they will love and respect us more for showing them the boundaries and caring enough for them to enforce the boundaries.

The truth is that we must be able to tell the difference between adolescent awkwardness and absentmindedness and sinful, rebellious behavior. We dare not let rebellion lodge in our youth's heart, nor let sinful destructive behavior take root. These must be dealt with diligently whether in a family or in a youth group. For instance, drinking and abusing drugs is not the result of absentmindedness or awkwardness, except as it relates to the adolescent's naivety, lack of judgment about who to be with, and their need to be accepted. Likewise, sneaking out of the house at night or rebellious backtalk must be dealt with head-on. There are dangers and temptations in the youth culture that, if not confronted immediately and decisively, can entrap the youngster for the rest of his or her life.

Adolescent development is a long process, not a sudden awakening. Even after Jesus' spiritual breakthrough and sense of call from His heavenly Father, His parents continued to oversee His further development. We read in verse 51 that after the incident at the temple in Jerusalem:

> *He went down with them and came to Nazareth, and He continued in subjection to them.*

Luke 2:51

We see this happened even after the incident at the temple where Jesus showed that He was leaving childhood behind and expressing greater independence. Yet His parents continued to parent Him and set His boundaries. Many parents today withdraw oversight and boundaries after several collisions with their child's new sense of independence. *One of the great disservices we do to our teenagers is to turn loose of them at the very time that they need us most.* At the exact moment when our kids need advice, counsel, encouragement and oversight, many parents withdraw from close involvement in their child's life. Many times it's because the parents feel ill equipped to deal with what their child is going through or fear conflicts with their teen. Many parents are afraid of reliving the chaos and pain they experienced growing up as an adolescent in their parents' home. However, this need not be since the Bible can give them understanding that their parents never had. The Bible also gives counsel and directions to both the parent and child to ensure that there is peace and blessing in the home even during the childhood and adolescent years.

When is the proper time to withdraw the boundaries and over-sight that we have over our kids? When should we give them greater freedoms? The answer, of course, is that we do so gradually, as they demonstrate their responsibility and ability to make biblical decisions even when faced with pressure and temptations.

Developing in Three Arenas

Let us make one last observation about the model of adolescent development that we see in Jesus. In the final verse of this passage we come across a summary statement that encapsulates what happened in the rest of His adolescent period.

And Jesus kept increasing in wisdom and stature, and in favor with God and man.

Luke 2:52

This very short verse says a lot about our strategy in dealing with adolescents. Here we see Jesus growing and increasing in the three arenas of adolescent development.

Arena One: "Wisdom And Stature"

This refers to the emotional, intellectual, and character development that must take place in the mind and soul of the developing adolescent. Merely focusing on school homework will not develop a successful, complete adult. There must be a clear plan to help the youth to develop good character as well. Likewise, participation in sports by itself will do little to develop good character. In fact, a recent study reported in *Teacher Magazine* found that high school athletes drank alcohol earlier and more often and began having sex at a younger age than non-athletes. Church and family are the most consistent and reliable developers of

84

character in youth, and their priority in the life of a young person must be guarded. Likewise, we must help our youth to have the counsel and feedback to help them deal with the emotional changes and stresses that come with adolescence. Getting adequate adult feedback is one of the greatest needs of adolescence and one that is often sadly lacking.

Arena Two: "Favor With God"

This speaks of the youth's spiritual development. Few adolescents have anyone that is seriously concerned about their faith development. *Our culture places great stress on education and intellectual development but very little on spiritual development.* Even physical development is of great concern in our culture. Physical education classes are a part of our kid's education, but there is no thought of spiritual education. There is a huge investment in sporting programs. Many parents will never miss a soccer or baseball game, but those same parents will never take their child to church.

This imbalance is especially evident in high school where football, wrestling, and basketball coaches make huge demands of the student's time. Parents gladly acquiesce to this. Many times, even minimal involvement in a church's youth program is dropped because of the excessive demands of high school sports.

This is a fatal mistake for parents who love their children. It has been demonstrated that involvement in church will greatly reduce a teen's likelihood of becoming involved in substance abuse or sexual activity and other dangerous behaviors, yet sports, as we saw above, will not. In fact, my brother John and I have often discussed the sad fact that success in high school sports almost invariably leads to teens eventually dropping out of church. We have noted very few exceptions to this rule, and, as we have sadly observed, very few return to church even after graduation.

Arena Three: "Favor With Man"

This third arena has to do with the development of a healthy social identity and social skills. Youth must learn how to interact with others in appropriate and positive ways. They must come to see their value, that is, how they contribute something that is valued by others.

Too many of our youth become crippled by peer dependence due to a lack of having a healthy self image. *Kids whose unique personalities and gifts are not identified and affirmed have no sense of who they are. They go in search of an identity.* Here positive but accurate adult feedback (not empty praise) is essential. When they are not affirmed by adults, then their only identity comes from the acceptance of their peers. More often than not, such acceptance requires foolish, immoral, ungodly or dangerous behavior.

We must work with our youth to help them discover the gifts and abilities they have and how they can contribute. We must help every young person discover for themselves the biblical truth that they are uniquely gifted with a unique and necessary part to play. In addition, we must offer them opportunities to excel and prove themselves.

A part of growing up is testing and proving themselves in new arenas. Young people need to succeed and gain the sense of mastery and social prestige that comes from excelling in challenging new endeavors. For many teenagers, the only place to test themselves and gain that prestige is school. However, if a young person fails to excel at classroom academics or sports, they will tend to have a damaged self-image or be driven to negative, socially destructive behavior in order to gain a needed sense of identity and potency.

86

We, as parents and churches, must take the time to know our kids, discover their gifts and strengths, and introduce them to places where they can shine. This must include challenging our young people with opportunities to do significant ministry, including opportunities in foreign missions.

The Critical Years

Adolescence is one of the most important phases of human life. It requires great attention and care on the part of parents and churches. Any observer of society can see that Satan gives this period great attention. There is a great effort aimed at winning the hearts and minds of this age group. Huge industries have arisen to entrap these youth in dangerous and addicting behavior, thereby robbing them of their future and destiny. Pitched battles are fought over control of their education because whatever they believe and whatever they value during this period will set the course for the rest of their life.

It has been my observation after nearly thirty years of ministry that the years of twenty-two to forty-five are largely just a postscript to decisions that were made between the ages of thirteen to twenty-one. If wise and godly choices were made, then they enter adult life prepared and with a good start, and they will most likely enjoy a good and happy life. If not, they may spend several decades trying to recover from addictions and dependencies. They may pay child support and watch some other man raise their child. They may have a prison record. They may have a lack of adequate education. The list is almost endless. Most of my counseling with adults is the result of problems that are rooted in bad choices made during the teen years.

Today's children and youth are available to whoever values and pursues them the most. Businessmen who value the dollars that youth have in their pocket go to great lengths to understand youth and try to win their hearts and affections. They do this because they want the kids' money. Apparently they value the kids' money more than most churches value their eternal souls since these greedy businessmen work so much harder to win them. We have what the youth of today want and desperately need. Many of them will choose Christ if we will become patient and loving guides.

9

The Four Questions of Adolescence

The period of adolescence (ages eleven to seventeen) is a time of intense questioning. This is according to the Creator's plan. The young person is finally able to ask questions that must be faced before one can become a person of conviction. This process is important because God desires that all people live by convictions rather than simply reacting to pressures and temptations.

There are four basic questions all adolescents struggle to answer. *The first question is one of identity.*

Who Am I?

Remember, they're going through great changes physically, intellectually, and emotionally. The body of an adult is replacing the body of a child. New, unsettling questions are bubbling up in their minds. Things that used to satisfy and interest them no longer do. Understand that these changes were uninvited and are largely beyond their control. Since they are surrounded by a peer group who are themselves struggling with these same changes, there is great turmoil and upheaval in their social world as well.

New changes are taking place quite rapidly. Everything seems to be changing. The youths can't help but wonder, "Who am I anyway?" They are changing, but what are they becoming? The result of all this is great confusion and insecurity. They become preoccupied with their physical appearance since they want to put on a good show outside that will hide the confusion and insecurity inside. Hours are spent in front of the mirror or at the gym. Great effort is spent to cover up for any perceived deficiency. Their current insecurity makes every supposed defect overwhelming to them.

At the same time, they have a new ability to do abstract thinking and look at themselves, their home, and how they were raised in a more detached and objective way. They are assaulted with new, pressing questions. Just how normal are they? How normal was their home life? Is there anything wrong with them? What do others think of them? How do they fit into the world? How are they like other people? How are they different? Do they have abilities that make them unique?

The next question is largely a result of their new intellectual abilities. *The second question is one of belief.*

What Do I Believe?

The youth is now, for the first time, fully able to consider the competing claims of other philosophies and religions. Just what is the truth? Should I believe something just because it's what I have been taught? Are the answers that I have grown up with right? It's not rebellion to ask these questions but a necessary part of becoming a person of conviction. This process, however, becomes especially traumatic and dangerous in today's world. Through various means, what Christian children have been taught at home and church is being systematically and skillfully undermined. As a result, unless Christian parents are vigilant and discerning, a great many of their children may not adopt the belief system of their parents, or they will give it only nominal ascent.

The next question is *a question of belonging.*

Who Do I Relate To? Where Do I Belong?

Just as in the story of Jesus and His parents, the young person is having an increasingly difficult time relating to his or her parents. Relationships are changing, and it's difficult to keep equilibrium between parents and child. There is a saying that a boy becomes a man two years later than he thinks he does and two years earlier than his dad thinks he does. Youth think they are ready for certain challenges and freedoms sooner than their parents do. Such a difference in perspectives is bound to bring with it misunderstanding and sometimes even conflict.

Their friends, however, do share the same perspective. Unlike their parents, the adolescents feel that their friends understand them since they are going through the same things. This explains the long hours spent with their friends on the phone or in chat rooms. Every evening they try to figure out and process what went on that day with their trusted confidants. Probably at no other time in life are friends so important to a person. *The problem is that at the same time they are making life-defining choices, their primary counselors are their peer group.* Unfortunately, these "counselors" do not have any more experience or know any more than they do. One of the most successful strategies we can have in training up our adolescents in the way they should go is by helping to make sure that they have a positive, godly peer group. We do this by supervising where they spend their free time.

In addition to their friends, they can also relate to a few non-family adults. The adolescent needs to look outside the family system for affirmation and feedback. This is part of the individuation process we looked at earlier. Favorite teachers, coaches, and youth workers become new mirrors to help the youth to see and understand themselves as well as being additional role models to the parents.

91

When all else fails and the young person feels misunderstood or alienated, they will withdraw into their room and relate only to themselves, listening to headphones, watching television, or reading a book.

The question of belonging is a central one to them, and they will work hard to belong to a "tribe." Because they have entered adolescence, their relationship with their family is changing. They are being prepared for the time when they will leave the family to go out and begin their own lives. This is God's plan, not the child's decision. They know that they will never belong to their parents and family in quite the same way again. So just where do they belong? Life is slowly but inexorably pushing them out of the nest, but where do they fit in? This is a burning question for them and explains why they will go to such extreme lengths in appearance and behavior in order to belong to some gang or subgroup. The very worst thing for an adolescent is to be an outcast. It tells him the one thing he doesn't want to hear: he doesn't belong anywhere.

The last question they seek an answer to is a *question of competence.*

Do I Have What It Takes?

Youth realize when they have once and for all left childhood behind. Up ahead is adulthood with all of its challenges and demands. Do they have what it takes to succeed in that world? The adolescent is forever testing and pressing themselves for the answer to that question. They desperately hope the answer is yes and will work very hard to prove that they have what it takes.

It's amazing to watch the passion with which high school students will throw themselves into sports, drama, or some other extracurricular program. Twice daily practices, six or seven days a week in stifling heat, are willingly done in the early part of the football season. Students who want to be on the football team will exert themselves until they are physically sick. Students will stay up all night to maintain a certain grade point average. They will do this because they have something to prove. Many boys who do not excel at some of these early tests like sports or academics will soon drop out and try to excel at some other perhaps dangerous and deviant form of proving themselves. They may try to prove themselves with violence, drug abuse, or reckless behavior. *Although these behaviors are dangerous, anything is better than thinking that you don't have what it takes.*

It's so important at this point in their life that they find some special ability, talent, or skill that will give them a sense of competence and personal empowerment. For some, they will find this in school, but for others, the answer will not be found inside the traditional program of the high school but perhaps in an outside job or volunteer position.

For those of us who work with youth it's important that we recognize these four basic questions and help our students to gain God's answers for them. If we do not provide God's answers, there will certainly be those eager to provide different answers.

Answering the Question, "Who Am I?"

Let's look at the answers the Bible gives to these four questions and how we can help our youth to find and accept them. First let's look at God's answer to the question of identity: WHO AM I?

Our students are taught in school that they are just a highly evolved animal. They are the product of a series of accidents or mutations and owe their existence to nothing more than random processes and blind chance.

We must make sure that they understand what the Bible teaches about them. It teaches that the human race is no accident but rather the centerpiece in a wonderful plan that the Creator of the universe is bringing to pass. He has made us in His own image so that we can know Him and reflect His glory.

Even more wonderful is the fact that each of us is of great importance and interest to our Creator. The Bible teaches us that even before we were born God knew us and was working to develop us in our mother's womb.

This is what the Lord says, He who made you, who formed you in the womb, and who will help you: "Do not be afraid."

Isaiah 44:2, NIV

God tells each person they are important to Him. He knows them as individuals and is committed to them, and therefore they do not need to be afraid. He has promised to be their helper. However, the Bible goes even further.

Thank you for making me so wonderfully complex! Your workmanship is marvelous – how well I know it. You watched me as I was being formed in utter seclusion, as I was woven together in the dark of the womb. You saw me before I was born. Every day of my life was recorded in your book. Every moment was laid out before a single day had passed. How precious are your thoughts about me, O God. They cannot be numbered!

Psalm 139:14-17, NLT

Not only did God know us and give us life in our mother's womb but He also developed a purpose and plan for each life. Our lives has been fully thought through by Him. He knows every day that we will live, and He has given great thought to each of us.

So many young people I meet today believe that their birth was unplanned or unwanted. Many of their parents were clearly unprepared to raise them. Many young people are shuttled and moved around and even raised by grandparents. They can't help but feel that they are an unplanned inconvenience. However, *Psalm 139:14-17 tells us there are no unplanned or unwanted children. Each person was planned for and welcomed by God, and He has made an unbreakable commitment to them.*

After sharing this truth with young people many hundreds of times, it's still one of the greatest thrills of my life. It's amazing to watch their response when they grasp this truth. In our Youth Venture Teen Centers we work with over 90 percent unchurched youth. Central to our YV program is our mentoring course. These are individual lessons that an adult takes an adolescent through one on one. The first lesson is called, "So What...Who Cares?" and is a lesson on identity and motivation. In it we teach them this concept of God's foreknowledge and plan for them. It has a powerful impact on almost every young person I have ever taken through it, no matter what their background. You can see hope come into them and fill them. You can see it in their eyes. It's like watching your breath fill up a balloon.

Just think, each of them is uniquely loved by the greatest being in the universe. He has made each of them unique, right down to their fingerprints. Each is different with different gifts and differing dreams because God has a unique plan for each. If they will follow God, He will show each of them their place in life and will become their life partner. The youth is freed from trying to measure up to some ideal or prototype in youth culture in order to gain an identity. They can now receive it as a gift that slowly unwraps as they get to know and follow God.

Young people thrill as they realize that God will be their life partner. Even if many others have abandoned or forsaken them, God has made an unbreakable commitment.

Though my father and mother forsake me, the Lord will receive me.
Psalm 27:10, NIV

I will never desert you, nor will I ever forsake you.
Hebrews 13:5

Nothing in all creation will ever be able to separate us from the love of God.
Romans 8:39, NLT

These are the truths that we must make sure to share with our young people as they begin to ask the question of identity, WHO AM I? These are the truths that will give them a foundation to build on.

Answering the Question, "What Do I Believe?"

The next question we must help them answer is a question of belief: WHAT DO I BELIEVE? The "faith" they had as an eight or nine-year-old is no longer sufficient. They are now able to ask new questions, and we must be ready to address these questions. The Christian faith has the best, most complete, and most satisfying answers to the questions of life of any competing religion or philosophy. We must take care to help our young people as they search and question. We must remember that for those in public school, they are being supplied every day with answers that contradict the answers of the

Bible. The kids are rewarded at school in a variety of ways if they accept these other answers. They need our support and help.

The worldview they are taught is that everything has gotten here by random processes and blind chance (evolution). This means there is no designer and therefore no design. There is no plan, and no transcendent purpose to life. In school every subject is approached *as if* there is no God (agnosticism). Everything is explained without ever referring to God.

Because there is no Creator—just random processes—and therefore no plan, there can be no absolute right and wrong (relativism). If there is no absolute right and wrong and no plan then there is nothing more important than to experience pleasure and make myself happy (hedonism). I should take pleasure wherever I find it.

With no Creator and no absolute standard, there is nothing higher than the individual (subjectivism). Self-esteem becomes the highest good and the new religion. It alone will produce positive change since it will release the ultimate good, which is the good within me. I am the measure of what is true for me. I should therefore resist any code or authority outside myself, even the Bible. The rights of every individual, even those of the child over the parent, become paramount. Nothing should restrict the freedom of the individual to do whatever pleases him or her. Whatever tries to do so is dangerous or evil, even Christianity! Without any ultimate goal or guarantees in life, living for the present moment becomes the logical thing to do (existentialism). All of the above brings us to this conclusion: *I should act in whatever way necessary to get as much personal pleasure out of this moment for myself as possible.*

This is what kids are taught in school and in popular media, and this is why young people in America act as they do. Whenever I see

97

youth looking and acting out of control, I always ask myself, "How would I act if I had grown up in their family and only been taught what they were taught in public school and popular media?" I might be doing exactly the same thing.

Young people today deserve better answers than these. Unless we supply a better, more compelling worldview, they will continue to live out the one outlined above. We must supply scientifically supported biblical answers for such issues as the origin of the world, human sexuality, biblical authority, comparative religions, stewardship, etc. In some cases this will mean having seminars and bringing in outside speakers or joining with other churches that are large enough to schedule such things. We must not fall into the trap of just entertaining our children and youth. We should not be afraid of boring them by getting into heavy topics. Our young people are hungry for answers. Remember what we saw earlier. Whatever a person comes to believe during his adolescence is what they will probably believe all of their life.

Experiencing God in Worship

The answers they are seeking are more than just intellectual arguments. They need to experience the spiritual reality behind the intellectual doctrines of our faith. They need to be brought to a point of encounter with spiritual truth. We need to bring them to spiritual experience with the three members of the Trinity. Through worship, Bible teaching, prayer, and the laying on of hands, we can help them see and feel the truth of what the Bible says.

At our church we have found that teaching our children and youth to worship is essential to getting them to choose the Bible's answers for life. Worship is at the center of all that we do in our children's and youth ministry. We teach our children to have in-depth worship experiences with the Lord. Some of my favorite memories are those with hundreds of children and youth and seeing them caught up into God's presence through worship. It's an awesome, life-changing experience.

In addition we have found that camps and retreats are essential parts of our strategy. Many people point to a camp experience as one of the spiritual highpoints of their life. Perhaps you are one of them. The seclusion and unhurried time at camp allows people to focus on God. They can experience the spiritual power and truth of what they have been taught.

Even though I am a senior pastor, I still attend and speak at six youth camps every year. In addition, each year we run a major three day youth conference called Future Quest. In this conference, as well as all of our camps, prolonged worship and soaking prayer is a major part of the program. Our church probably spends more on these camps and this conference than any other budget item outside of staff salaries, mortgages, and missions. This is because these are the best times for our children and youth to experience the power behind the truths they are being taught.

Answering the Question, "Where Do I Belong?"

The third question we must help them answer is the question of belonging: WHO DO I RELATE TO? WHERE DO I BELONG?
In order to truly help our young people, the church must recover our sense of being a family. An adolescent who is part of a loving and accepting church family will have far less difficulty with this question. This is such an important issue that I have devoted the next chapter to it.

Small Groups

One way we can help our youth in search of a place to belong is to develop a small-group ministry that allows different niches for the young person to fit into. At our church, each group is unique and allows each young person to find a small group with which they have an affinity. If we only offer a large, high-energy youth meeting, we ensure that many young people will not feel they fit or belong there. Large groups of young people tend to form cliques that are very hard to penetrate. There's usually a very rigid pecking order in place.

With enough small groups every young person should find a place where he or she is accepted. Small groups tend to sort out according to common interests and preferences. At our church, many high school-aged young people who either don't like or feel accepted at our large weekly meeting participate in one of our twenty-four small groups. Of course, many students participate in both the big meeting and the small groups.

Adult Mentors

A second way to help our young people develop a sense of belonging is to develop relationships between them and older church members. In our case, much of this comes from the small groups where long-term relationships are built with the adults who lead or participate. In addition, we have intentional programs to match youth with mentors and have developed mentoring materials for them to go through together. We will explore this in depth later.

We teach our children and young people that as soon as they accept Christ as their Lord and Savior, they become a part of our family. Each of us is related because all of us have the same

Father in heaven. Furthermore, we tell them we are "blood relatives" because all of us are related by the blood of Jesus. These are more than mere words to us. We treat these children and youth as though they really are a part of our family. On many occasions I've heard our young refer to our church as their "family." My own three boys grew up at our church, and they think of dozens of people as uncles, aunts, and grandparents. Many of our Youth Venture and Bus Ministry kids have lived for weeks, months, and even years with our church members due to their distressed family situations.

Answering the Question, "Do I Have What It Takes?"

The fourth question we must help them with is the question of competency. This is the question: DO I HAVE WHAT IT TAKES? Do I have the competency and the power to succeed in life? Do I have the talents and gifts to contribute something important? Will I measure up and find a place where I will matter?

The church is the ideal place for our young people to discover gifts and talents and be able to test themselves. This is because the church is the greatest user of volunteer help in the world. Every healthy church has a multifaceted variety of places to serve. The church can employ virtually any gift and any talent. The church offers training, supervision, and encouragement. In addition, the church holds as a conviction that every life has a purpose and every person has a necessary gift to contribute.

> *As **each one** has received a special gift, employ it in serving one another as good stewards of the manifold [i.e. many forms] grace of God.*
> 1 Peter 4:10, emphasis mine

The Joshua Principle

*Since we have gifts that differ according to the grace given to us, **each of us** is to exercise them accordingly.*
Romans 12:6, emphasis mine

*But to **each one is given** the manifestation of the Spirit for the common good....But one and the same Spirit works all these things, distributing to each one individually just as He wills.*
1 Corinthians 12:7, 11, emphasis mine

God fills all people with the need to be fruitful or productive. It's part of our genetic makeup. We see it in Genesis when God blessed us and told us to "be fruitful and multiply and fill the earth and subdue it and rule." It further says that He planted a garden and put man in it to "cultivate and keep it." In order to have a good self-image, people must be productive. This is as true for adolescents as it is for adults. *Just like adults, kids need to be needed.*

In today's complex and often dangerous world, there are fewer and fewer opportunities for adolescents to contribute. Unlike the days when most families lived on the farm, children are not needed. Few families own their own businesses where their kids can develop skills and earn their wings, but the church *does* need them and offers them a meaningful job to do.

At our church we attempt to involve every young person in ministry and service, beginning in the sixth grade. We encourage our middle school to be involved in our Junior High Leadership Corps. This group serves the church and the community in a variety of ways and learns how fulfilling it is to be a servant leader. Even at this age our kids serve the younger grades. My thirteen-year-old son is in his second year as part of the Sunday morning team that ministers to the first and second graders. As they move into high school, the opportunities to minister increase. Some are leaders in our small group ministry. Others help in the after school Bible clubs at local elementary and middle schools. Four of the local public high schools have Christian clubs in which students from our church are leaders. In addition, others serve in our bus ministry. The list goes on and on.

We give them opportunities to serve, be needed and discover and develop their God-given gifts and talents. They learn confidence and develop an identity and a sense of personal potency. Such young people are far less dependent on the approval of peers. They have greater confidence to go their own way. Remember, one of our main jobs as older Christians is to prepare the next generation to be fruitful and to be leaders.

No one has such good news to give to kids who are asking, "Do I have what it takes?" We can assure them that they are uniquely gifted by God and that God will become their partner to accomplish the destiny He has ordained for them.

For we are His workmanship, created in Christ Jesus for good works, which God prepared beforehand so that we would walk in them.
Ephesians 2:10

I can do all things through Him who strengthens me.
Philippians 4:13

For it is God who is at work in you, both to will and to work for His good pleasure.
Philippians 2:13

The Joshua Principle

10

It Takes a Family

I magine the scene around Jesus' cross. He is in agony as His life is slipping away. Surrounding Him is a group of women who, because of their lesser status in society, were not considered a threat and were allowed to approach the cross. Standing a little farther off at a safe distance amid the crowd are some of Jesus' disciples, including John, who often refers to himself in his Gospel merely as "the disciple that Jesus loved." In the midst of this scene Jesus raises His head, gathers His strength, and speaks.

> *When Jesus then saw His mother, and the disciple whom He loved standing nearby, He said to His mother, "Woman behold your son!" Then He said to the disciple, "Behold your mother!" From that hour the disciple took her into his own household.*
>
> John 19:26-27

This is what Jesus does. He takes people who are not related by blood or genetics and He makes them a family. It's not just that He makes them like a family. He does more. He makes them into family. From that day, we read, John took Mary home to his house and took responsibility for her as a good son would for his mother.

God's Model for a Family

How should we think of the church? What should be our model in building it? Pastors run from conference to conference in search of the latest, cutting-edge model. But what is Jesus' model? What is the Bible's model?

Paul writes to Timothy, reminding him of the essence of the church.

*I write so that you will know how one ought to conduct himself in **the household of God, which is the church** of the living God, the pillar and support of the truth.*
1 Timothy 3:15, emphasis mine

The church is the pillar and support of the truth, but before it can be that it must be something else. It must be a family. It's the very household or family of God. Jesus said that all those who do the will of God are His brothers, sisters, and mothers (Matthew 12:48-50). If you read that passage, you will see that Jesus gave the bonds of spiritual family priority over the bonds of physical family. In other words, being part of God's family has a greater call on our life than does our biological family.

Paul told Timothy that all interactions in the church should be conducted on the basis of family because, first and foremost, that is what we are.

Do not sharply rebuke an older man, but rather appeal to him as a father, to the younger men as brothers, the older women as mothers, and the younger women as sisters, in all purity.
1 Timothy 5:1-2

This is the essence of church. Notice in the passage above that the church, like every other family, must be intergenerational, that is, it must be made up of people of different ages. Fathers, mothers, sons, daughters, and even grandparents make up a family. *A church must be a family or it is not a church; it has become something else.* Being family is not merely an ideal to talk about in a sermon but a reality that we must be living out. Every church must act and feel like a family.

Family is very important in God's plan. It was His first invention after resting on the seventh day following creation. He made a mate for Adam and told them to be fruitful and multiply—or to make a family—and then take dominion (Genesis 2:18, 21-24). Four out of the Ten Commandments deal directly with family. God even chose a family title for Himself. He tells us to call Him Father.

God's greatest works have taken place through a man and his family. It all began with Adam and his family. Then, when the world grew wicked, God preserved the human race through one man, Noah, and his family. He chose a man, Abraham, and his family to begin His redemptive purposes, giving them covenant promises that would bless all mankind. The promise of a future Messiah/Savior was given to King David and his family. Now God continues to work through a family. That family is the church with Jesus as its head. A church must be a family or else it isn't a church; it has become something else. We cannot succeed unless we take seriously God's plan that the church is a family.

The Power of Family

Why is family so important to God? Because a family is the matrix in which healthy human souls are to develop. Family is God's design to develop people who can become His godly sons and daughters. Nothing else will affect a person's life as much as his or her family. That is the God-given power of family. There is no program, institution, or governmental agency that can either equal its power or undo its effect. Family is simply determinative in a way that nothing else is.

There is no plan B. There is nothing beyond the family that can do the families' job. Family marks a person's life like nothing else. A dysfunctional family wounds a person in a way that troubles them all their life.

After thirty years of ministry, I have learned that people *live out what they learned in their family until they become part of another family that does it differently.* Usually, only then does it become possible for them to truly change. It takes the power of a new family to help mitigate the damage of the first family and bring that human soul to maturity. This is the power of a church that functions as a family. Counseling programs that aren't linked to the power of family have very limited effect.

Understanding all of this will change our approach to ministering to children and youth. Youth ministry cannot merely be another program that the church offers. Instead, it's a sacred parenting responsibility. When God touches a young person's heart, He brings them into His family, the church. He gives them what every young person yearns for and needs most. He gives them a family. He calls on a local church family to open up their hearts and adopt one more child. This responsibility is not discharged merely by going on the internet and hiring some "youth ministry specialists" who have put their résumés into cyberspace.

Back to the Future

One of the great needs in the church is to recover the family model of ministry. The church has largely adopted the modern concept of *mass* marketing, *mass* communication, and *mass* manipulation. It's tempting to try to reach people *en masse*, especially when you consider the numbers that must be reached. However, it doesn't work. People don't change en masse but rather individually. The tools that bring about deep, lasting change in people's lives are not a television show, book, crusade, or rally. It's a family. There is a place for all of these other things, but they can't replace family in God's plan.

Only one thing can bring a young person to the full, godly maturity that God intends for them. That one thing is a spiritual family, one that truly loves him, that is committed to his present and future well-being, and that will exercise discipline and accountability over him. *For many young people, church will be their only real chance to belong to a family.*

Kids today desperately need families. Nothing has so negatively impacted the younger generation as much as the breakup of the family in America, and nothing can restore that generation as much as offering them a new, spiritual family. Social scientists used to debate the cause of juvenile delinquency, teen pregnancy, alcohol and drug abuse, and school drop-out rates. Was it poverty, discrimination, or environment, they wondered?

Today, the debate is over. Every study agrees. The single biggest predictor of all these crises among our youth is the condition of the student's family, especially the presence or absence of a father in the home. The plagues affecting our young people, like gangs, substance abuse, and teen suicide, are all rooted in family problems. Gangs become surrogate families, and drugs become dangerous replacements for the missing comfort and support of absent or dysfunctional parents, many who are themselves battling addiction or alcoholism. Unlike the parents, the drugs are always there, and they can always be counted on.

What Every Young Person Wants

Every young person needs a good family to grow up with, and every young person wants loving and competent mothers and fathers. God's answer is the church. He fathers the fatherless through placing them in His spiritual family.

A Father for the fatherless and a judge for the widows, is God in His holy habitation. God makes a home for the lonely.

Psalm 68:5-6

The NKJV translates that last line:

God sets the solitary in families.

In this verse God states that He is a Father to the fatherless, but then He also states that He is in His holy habitation (i.e., heaven). How, then, does God intend to fully father these fatherless who are here on earth? God's plan is right there in the above verse. God places the lonely and solitary into spiritual families or local churches. Through the members of these local families/churches He can care for and father them.

Families are a deep need for all of us. Many women grieve over not being able to be mothers. Perhaps they were never married or were prevented from giving birth due to a physical or medical problem, and yet God's answer for them is in the church.

He makes the barren woman abide in the house as a joyful mother of children.

Psalm 113:9

"Shout for joy, O barren one, you who have born no child; break forth into joyful shouting and cry aloud, you who have not travailed; for the sons of the desolate

one will be more numerous that the sons of the married woman," says the Lord.

Isaiah 54:1

There are children for every barren woman in God's family. There are grandchildren for every elderly person. There is a father and mother, grandparents, and older brothers and sisters for every hurting and seeking youth in God's family if we will simply start operating like a family.

Unfortunately, instead of doing it God's way, we design our youth programs according to the humanistic model of public education. We isolate our youth into large youth ghettos overseen by a few professional "youth specialists" who are not much older than the youth. The results are by all accounts abysmal. It's not God's way.

While there is certainly a place for modern models of youth ministry, they must enhance and not replace the concept of spiritual family and intergenerational ministry. At our church we have weekly children's and youth meetings, full-time youth pastors, interns, youth camps, and a large youth conference. However, the heart and soul of our church's ministry to youth is formed around relationships of those youth with caring and loving adults.

Spiritual Family Based Youth Ministry

Our junior high ministry, for instance, although very large, is built around a spiritual family dynamic. Almost fifteen years ago as our junior high ministry was growing, my brother John, our youth pastor, and I were troubled by the limitations of trying to minister to a large group of kids. It was also apparent that we were wasting our adult helpers since they didn't have any important role to play. They

111

seemed unfulfilled as they stood by and watched one or two people do the entire ministry. We came up with a new approach that has served us well all these years.

Our entire junior high youth group meets only once a month. During the other weeks they meet in nineteen smaller groups of fifteen to twenty-five members, all of the same sex. These function, in effect, as individual youth groups. They are overseen by two or more adults, and many of them have high school helpers as well. These leaders are responsible to oversee the weekly fun activity, lead the Bible teaching, and facilitate discussion and worship.

As you can see, this model demands a high level of commitment from the adult leaders to the kids they lead. The kids in these groups stay together during the entire three years of middle school, although new kids may also join. Most leaders stay with the group during those three years. It's also not unusual for these leaders to stay with them as they move into high school. Some of these leaders are parents with a child in the group, but all of them act as surrogate parents and big brothers/sisters to all the kids. Trust and love are developed, and the participants form lifelong friendships not only with each other but also with the adults. Although we try to make the meetings fun, the main reason that the kids return week after week is because they know that they are loved.

We have eighty-five adults and high school helpers who work with our junior high ministry. People might wonder how we could find so many adults willing to make such a high commitment. The answer is that we are not asking them to volunteer to help with a program. We are not asking them to merely drive, blow up volleyballs, or help keep order while the youth pastor ministers. We are asking them to form loving relationships and invest their lives in young people. We are asking them to be part of a family and change a young person's life. We do not have difficulty finding volunteers to step forward. *People may burn out trying to make a program function, but they never burn out at being a family.*

Our high school ministry operates with similar values. Besides a large group meeting every Tuesday night, our students gather in twenty-four weekly small groups. These groups allow much leadership to be handled by the students themselves, but each group has a least one adult who is personally mentoring the leaders of the group. What we've found is that some students prefer the large group meeting, others go only to the smaller home fellowship gatherings, but most are involved in both. By taking this dual approach we are able to reach a wider range of students. All of our small group leaders, both student and adults, receive extensive support and mentoring by our Youth Pastor, John Hoffman. This includes both seminars and special retreats.

We operate our youth ministry this way because we operate our whole church this way. Our church has always been built around relationships, around mentoring, and around membership in small groups. Our whole church is built around intergenerational family type relationships and lay ministry.

Besides our church youth groups, we operate four commu-nity youth centers (open seven days a week) and twenty-three on-campus after school Bible clubs. Ten of these clubs are at area public elementary schools and are overseen by our Children's Pastor, Dan Deyling. The remaining thirteen clubs are at area public middle schools and are overseen by Pastor Dan Eslinger, who also oversees our four Youth Venture community youth centers. Both the afterschool Bible clubs and the youth centers are designed to reach unchurched kids. In fact, over 90 percent of the

113

several thousand children and youth who participate in these programs are from unchurched homes. All of these are operated upon the biblical concept of spiritual family. Is it successful? The answer is a huge yes. The kids come running by the hundreds because they were created for family. I hear all the time from our adult volunteers that they get as much or more out of it as the kids.

As you can imagine, all this requires several hundred volunteers to accomplish. How do we find them all in a church that averages 2,500, counting children, in attendance at the weekend services? Remember, this is on top of all the other need for volunteers that a church our size requires. The answer is that it has become the culture of our church. It's all done without strain and with joy. It's because we are a spiritual family, and in a family everyone contributes.

Seeing the Church as Family

To take God's plan for family seriously, our churches must do two things:

First, we must make it a priority to support, minister to and build up the families that belong to our church. This means that we must offer in-depth quality engagement and pre-marriage classes and counseling. It means we must provide or direct our people to marriage enrichment groups, marriage retreats, and biblical marriage counseling. It also means that we have regularly scheduled, Bible-based parenting seminars and have mature couples available to mentor others in marriage and parenting. If a church can't offer all of these, it can network with specialized ministries that offer these programs or use the resources of larger churches.

Second, we must take seriously what it means to have the church function on a spiritual family model. This might mean big changes for some churches. We must change the culture of the church to one of being a spiritual family. This has to start from the top. It has to come from the pulpit. It has to be received by the people in the pews.

We must understand that church is a family. It's not a slick event we put on every Sunday. If we truly live this out, it will, in the long run, build much stronger Christians and churches. It would bring about true and rapid church growth in a city because it would produce Christians who can multiply. This *multiplication* would soon far outstrip our attempts to *add* through our Sunday focused efforts. It would finally allow us to influence our culture.

Why have so many of our churches drifted so far from the concept of family? Why have so many churches been built on a different model? Perhaps the biggest answer is because our culture as a whole doesn't really value, encourage, or understand family. *Radical individualism, materialism, and feminism have destroyed family for many people.* As a result, few people today grow up in the kind of family that God intended. This is true for most people in our churches, even for many of our pastors. Most people have never grown up in a healthy family where mom and dad love God and each other, have a healthy marriage, understand their roles, are committed to their kids, and live biblical lives of maturity and integrity. We, therefore, have a hard time producing that kind of a family in our churches.

So, if our culture doesn't understand family, what does it understand? Well, we understand shopping malls and specialty stores that try to anticipate and cater to the latest whims of consumers. We flock to sports arenas and multiplex theaters that entertain us. The young frequent bars and clubs that cater to a narrow demographic clientele where everyone is the same age, looks the same, and has the same interests.

Unfortunately, church leaders who understand their culture very well, but apparently not their Bible, build their churches on these models, falsely believing that they are on the cutting edge. When we do this, we are leading people away from a true church experience. What we create may build attendance quickly, but it will not produce lasting changes in people. A church must be a family or else it isn't a church; it has become something else. If it isn't a family, it lacks the God-given power of family to bring people to wholeness and maturity.

If youth ministry is merely a program offered as part of a church's product line to attract and hold religious consumers, then the youth of that church will not be brought through to Christian maturity and wholeness. *Just like the head of a real family, the pastor of the church must be intimately involved in the care and development of the young.* It's not enough to merely hire a series of short-lived "youth ministry specialists" to "take care of the problem." He must be involved in overseeing the spiritual care of the young and vulnerable. In fact, I would argue that this is his highest responsibility as chief shepherd of the church.

Developing Mature Leaders

A pastor's goal should never be to have the largest or fastest growing church. It must be to produce a spiritually healthy family. After all, families are not races to see who can entice the greatest amount of people to sit around their dinner table. *Rather, they are gutsy, costly endeavors to bring children to birth, protect them, and then raise them to maturity and productivity.* When the process is complete, they go out and produce children of their own, and we have a multigenerational family. Dad becomes granddad and maybe later great-granddad. This must be the goal and pattern of God's spiritual families as well.

At Foothills we have attempted to live out this ideal. Since our first day we have never had to hire anyone from outside of our church to come on staff for any position. Even as we have experienced steady and sometimes rapid growth, we've never had to look beyond our own church family. At the very same time we have never had a staff member leave to assume a position at another church and have only had to let one staff member go in more than twenty years. These might seem like incredible facts for a church that had grown to 2,500 in worship attendance. The reason is we are a spiritual family. We do not attempt to grow faster than leadership can organically arise from within. In fact, many of our most effective staff members found Christ right here at Foothills. *We make caring for and developing the people God gives us a priority rather than looking for a shortcut to explosive Sunday morning attendance growth.* When we do bring someone into leadership, we work with them to make them effective even if their performance is weak at the beginning. That's how you treat family!

In addition to our church, we have developed leaders for our two schools (both of our principals are products of our church, as are most of the teachers), a drug and alcohol recovery ranch, and a church plant, as well as all our various outreaches. In addition, we have sent some of our interns to serve at other churches and ministries. This can only happen because we make leadership development a priority.

We who are pastors must reject the current measure of success, which is weekend attendance at worship services. This is unbiblical and shortsighted. Such a focus is actually hurting the cause of Christ. It's producing immature Christians and setting the overall advance of the church back. Our measure of success must be the number of mature Christians we are producing who are themselves reproducing.

We must see every child growing up in our midst and every new convert as a future leader. We must believe in their God-given potential and be committed to their full development. We must be willing to make the investment to bring them to maturity and productivity, even if that process has a few setbacks. After all, isn't that how you treat your family members?

As you shall shortly see, we practice this philosophy at every level of youth ministry beginning in middle school. As a result, we not only have a number of new, young staff at our church and schools but we have also produced many young volunteer leaders and have raised up more than forty paid interns in the last ten years. We currently have thirteen, all products of our church.

11

Bridging the Gap

A sad fact has been noted and commented on in recent years. Although huge amounts of money have been spent on evangelism and church growth strategies, and even though fads and conferences have promoted new models for the church and new ways to "do church," and mega churches have sprouted up across the country like mushrooms, the overall church attendance has not increased, and our efforts to impact our culture for Christ have been mixed at best. *In many cases the culture seems to be evangelizing the church, and we are becoming more like it rather than the culture becoming more Christian.* How are we to explain this lack of success?

Certainly, two of the biggest reasons for this failure are that first, **we have not targeted our evangelism and discipleship to those who are especially prepared by God's design to respond (i.e., children and youth).** We have instead targeted those we think are more important and who will "pay off" sooner.

Secondly, when we do win a child, or an adult for that matter, to Christ, we bring them into our churches, which increasingly are program-driven institutions built around a business model rather than spiritual families. We have focused on short-term attendance growth rather than on the growth of God's Kingdom. I have written more on this subject in my book *On Earth As It Is in Heaven.*

Valuing Young People

First, let's look at whom we target for evangelism and ministry. In following our own wisdom we have done the very thing that Jesus told us not to do. We have despised or undervalued the young.

And He called a child to Himself and set him before them, and said, "Truly I say to you, unless you are converted and become like children, you will not enter the kingdom of heaven....And whoever receives one such child in My name receives Me; but whoever causes one of these little ones who believe in Me to stumble, it would be better for him to have a heavy millstone hung around his neck, and to be drowned in the depth of the sea....See that you do not despise one of these little ones, for I say to you that their angels in heaven continually see the face of My Father who is in heaven."
Matthew 18:2-3, 5-6, 10, emphasis mine

Let's remember the context of these words. The disciples had just asked Jesus who was the greatest in His Kingdom. Jesus took this child and set him before them. They must become like the child, He said. Read again the verses above and hear what Jesus is saying. **His Kingdom would be built with children and those who would become like them.** Therefore, they must make a place for the children and welcome them. They must carefully protect them and never neglect, despise, or treat them as unimportant. As we have already shown, *children would be at the center of His plan.*

And yet, if we are honest, we must admit that the church has largely failed in this aspect. Ministry to children and youth, as we have already seen, doesn't even get a proportionate amount of a church's budget and staffing; it's generally the least paid and has the highest turnover. And instead of protecting our children, we have mostly entrusted their minds and souls to a hostile public education and popular media while we have pursued building bigger and nicer buildings than are necessary and created more programs that please the adults whom we value more.

The Problem with Institutions

Secondly, as stated above, when we do bring a new convert into church, it's often a program-driven church that more closely resembles a corporation or institution than a family. The problem, however, is that institutions can't really help people. Only spiritual families will bring people to spiritual maturity where they can themselves reproduce.

Charles Simpson[16] has made the point that institutions never save people. He has noted, for instance, that hospitals don't save people; doctors and nurses do. Likewise, it's not churches that save and restore people but God working through the individual members of that church. Institutions and bureaucracies don't care for individuals, but families do. *It makes a huge difference whether we build our churches to be institutions or families.*

Recently I got a call from several eighth and ninth graders from one of our Youth Ventures. They wanted to know if they could come over and spend the night with us. Partially it was because they were bored and partially it was because they have difficult homes. Now, to some people raised in a different type of church, it might seem strange for neighborhood kids to call the senior pastor of a large church to see if they could sleep over at his house. But it didn't seem strange to them to call, and it didn't seem strange to my wife, me, or our kids to be asked. Over the years, our kids have grown accustomed to this happening. It might be strange if I'm a CEO of an

[16]Noted conference speaker and editor of *One on One* magazine.

institution, but not if I'm a father of a family. We had guests that night, so we couldn't let them. However, they have slept over in the past, and they will again in the future. That's how families operate.

Creating the Right Culture

This is the norm, not the exception, at our church. It has become our culture; our adults love all of our children and youth. All three of my sons have benefited greatly because of the relationships they each have with dozens of adults. We care for each other's kids. My children feel they have grown up in one huge family with many aunts and uncles and even grandparents.

The problem is so much of ministry is aimed at young people is primarily an institutional program. It's based around a regular meeting that is highly structured and platform centered. Kids come and watch a talented "youth specialist" and perhaps a talented worship band perform from the stage. Perhaps there is also humor and high-energy games meant to entertain the kids. *Success is usually measured by how large the crowd is on any given night.*

Adult relationships are minimal with very little for interested adults to do. The youth pastor tends to be young and inexperienced in life, and they tend to come and go with great frequency, very few remaining for three or more years. In many cases, by the time a youth has gone through the church's middle and high school program, he or she may have seen three or four different youth pastors come and go.

But kids don't need institutions or programs. Kids need families. Kids need relationships. Kids need protectors and guides.

122

Kids need examples and champions and even heroes to emulate. Young people, and all of us actually, need fathers, mothers, uncles, aunts, and grandparents, not directors and CEOs.

Recently I got a panicked call from a fifteen-year-old boy who began attending our church after he got involved through our Youth Venture program. He and his younger brother had been riding bikes when his brother was injured after his bike hit an obstacle, and he was pitched over the handlebars. He suffered an apparent concussion and was acting strangely. He called me immediately for help, not because I am the founder and executive director of Youth Ventures, but because I have become like a father to him.

Entertaining a kid or even inspiring him or her is not enough. They need to be loved, parented, and discipled. This only takes place in a spiritual family. In a church that is a spiritual family, there is room for everyone to play a part.

If you step back and look at our church, you will see that it's composed of what I call a *"chain of care."* Everyone is receiving ministry, but each is also giving ministry as they are able. Many of our middle school students are involved in helping with the ministry to children in nursery through third grade. In addition, many are involved in our Middle School Leadership Corps. This group serves in many practical ways to people in and out of our church. Our high school students minister extensively to our fourth to sixth grade students and in our middle school ministry and afterschool clubs. Our college-age young people are the workhorses of the church, serving in all the ministries to youth and children, including the high school ministry. In return they receive mentoring by older adults. Our young people value and seek out older mentors to help them grow. This is how families operate. This is also the model for ministry laid out in the Bible.

Gen-X Churches?

What family is made up of just adolescent siblings without mothers and fathers or grandparents, not to mention little brothers and sisters? And yet today we see a movement to establish "Gen-X churches" or "youth churches." In fact, these are all the rage, the latest fad. But what does it say about our discernment when as church leaders we follow the lead of worldly marketing strategies and market the body of Christ and build churches based on demographic differences? Just like the so called "seeker-driven" churches of the boomers, these are another step in the wrong direction.

The fatal flaw in both of these types of churches is that they are built on peoples' tastes and lifestyle choices, not on the cross of Christ. They reflect the carnal reasoning of the so-called "church-growth experts" who speak of the "homogenous principle." This principle states the fact that churches grow fastest when its members are all of similar race, age, backgrounds, and tastes. This is merely to restate the old adage that "birds of a [similar] feather flock together." It recognizes that people are more comfortable when they don't have to cross any boundaries, face new challenges, or step out of their comfort zones. *Of course, it's equally self-evident that people who live that way will not grow.*

True Church Growth

These approaches are said to be attempts at producing "church growth." True church growth, however, cannot be measured by any one church's Sunday morning attendance numbers. Rather, Ephesians 4 gives us the goal and measure of true church growth.

And He gave some as apostles, and some as prophets, and some as evangelists, and some as pastors and teachers, for

*the equipping of the saints for the work of service, **to the building up of the body of Christ** [i.e., **true church growth**]; until we all attain to the unity of the faith, and of the knowledge of the Son of God, **to a mature man, to the measure of the stature which belongs to the fullness of Christ**...but speaking the truth in love, **we are to grow up in all aspects into Him who is the head, even Christ.***
Ephesians 4:11-13, 15, emphasis mine

This verse tells us that church expansion must be growth into all aspects of Christ. It must be growth into the fullness of Christ. It must be growth into His stature. The church as a whole, including every member, must grow into true Christlikeness. Such growth will reveal the power, wonder, and love of Christ. This and this alone will truly honor God and satisfy the human soul. Such growth only occurs through the cross of Christ. It does not come through pandering to the flesh, but through crucifying the flesh. *Carnal strategies to attract crowds will not accomplish this.* It will not produce disciples of Christ who manifest His reality. It will only gather and produce religious consumers. *Consumers gather, but only disciples follow.* They follow because they have seen Christ and their flesh has been dealt with.

Churches built on a wrong model may grow in attendance, but they lack the power of family to bring people to maturity. These churches are built on the wisdom of man, not the wisdom of God. They are reflections of the breakdown of family in our culture. Many people don't know what it means to belong to a family. They don't know its power. Rather than try to teach people what a family is, many simply pander to our culture's sense of rootlessness, alienation, isolation, and self-absorption by the churches they create. Many innovations in these new churches seem to be driven by marketing fads and trends rather than by revelation of the Holy

Spirit. Only the future will reveal the tragic consequences of preferring man's cleverness and wisdom to God's plan.

The Reality of Family

One thing is for sure about your family, not everyone in it is just like you. Not everyone is your age or shares all your tastes and preferences. *In fact, you don't even get to choose who is in your family.* Except for the choice of who you will marry, you have no choice over who your family is. You don't get to select who is born into it or pick your in-laws, but that is where the power of family lies. It lies in the difficulties and the opportunities that such differences bring. It's in facing and dealing with those differences that people grow and mature. It's love and commitment, not preferences or tastes that make a family.

The same is true of the family of God. You don't get to choose who is in it; God does. In fact, the true reality and power of the church is only developed and revealed in the facing and breaking down of natural prejudices and barriers (see Ephesians 2:12-19; Galatians 3:28). It's only then that we fully witness the love and reconciling power of Jesus. If our gatherings and fellowship are based only upon natural tastes and preferences, we do not need God's power. We become nothing more than a religious club. Following the "homogenous principal" and "target marketing" in our churches will impoverish us by robbing us of the depths of Jesus' power and love. It will, in the end, not only result in shallower Christians and churches but also in less evangelism. Our greatest evangelism occurs when the unsaved witness God's great reconciling love and power on display in the Church.

In addition, the maturing process of youthful Christians is not best served by segregating them from older, more experienced

Christians. To seclude them with people who have little more life experience or wisdom than they do is to ensure that they will merely fall prey to the pitfalls common to the young and inexperienced. After all, when we are only around people just like us, we will surely be unable to see the blind spots that we share with them and will approve things that those older and wiser would warn us against. Jesus warned us against the blind leading the blind (Matthew 15:14).

At the same time, Gen-X churches tend to remove young adults from some of their most fruitful ministry opportunities. In general, we are not most effective with our own peers. Rather, we are generally most effective with those who are a little younger and less experienced than ourselves. For this reason, people in their early twenties have a unique opportunity to impact the life of adolescents. They are absolutely key players in reaching this most strategic age. Young adolescents look toward those in their early twenties and not to older adults as role models. The fact is that these "tweens" and young adolescents attend their parent's churches, not churches targeted to reach only people in their twenties. Gen-X churches draw this irreplaceable asset away from youth ministry.

The Price of the Generation Gap

Do you remember how Israel was split in two and how the house of David lost authority over the northern half of the kingdom? It happened after the death of King Solomon when his son, Rehoboam, was in Shechem waiting to be crowned king over all Israel. In response to a request from the people, Rehoboam went to his father's advisors for advice. They gave him sound advice based upon their accumulated wisdom and experience in governing people.

However, because Solomon had been a neglectful father and had not brought Rehoboam up in his presence or that of his advisors, Rehoboam's heart was not with them. He had not learned to trust in them or their counsel. Instead he turned to his peers, the young men he had grown up with. Like many today, he was estranged from his elders and had become "peer dependent." They gave him the advice one would expect from brash and inexperienced young men. When the people returned, Rehoboam answered them harshly according to the counsel of the young men of his peer group. It was a decision that would cost Rehoboam greatly.

But he forsook the counsel of the elders which they had given him, and consulted with the young men who grew up with him and served him...Then Jeroboam and all the people came to Rehoboam on the third day as the king had directed, saying, "Return to me on the third day." The king answered the people harshly, for he forsook the advice of the elders which they had given him, and he spoke to them according to the advice of the young men...When all Israel saw that the king did not listen to them, the people answered the king, saying, "What portion do we have in David? We have no inheritance in the son of Jesse. To your tents, O Israel! Now look after your own house, David."

1 Kings 12:8,12-14,16

In other words, the northern tribes broke away from the dynasty, which had begun under King David. Israel would never be united again. In one day Israel went from being the greatest kingdom in the eastern world to being two weak and feuding countries: Israel and Judah. Rehoboam had squandered his inheritance. Israel lost her dominion and would be in constant threat of being overrun by her enemies. And it all happened because Solomon failed to guide and win the heart of his son. As a result, *Rehoboam had a "father- less spirit" and disinherited himself from what should have been his.*

All this was a fulfillment of the principle outlined in Malachi 4:6 that states that when the hearts of fathers are not toward the hearts of the children and the hearts of the children are not toward the fathers, then the whole land falls under a curse. When the older generation does not see empowering and training up the younger generation as its primary task and joy, and the younger generation does not honor and seek out the counsel and blessing of the older generation, then the society falls under a curse. This is certainly the case in American society. Family has broken down. A gap has formed between the generations. We see the destructive effects all around. What is needed today is the restoration of fatherhood and motherhood. What is needed is the restoration of family, and it must begin in the church.

We dare not follow society in fragmenting along so called "generational" lines. Secular marketers talk about *"Builders," "Busters," "Xers,"* and *"Millenials,"* ad naseum. They exaggerate superficial differences between people who are all alive at the same time. They do this in an attempt to widen such divisions in order to sell their product. But in the church such so-called generations shouldn't matter. What does matter is what "age" we belong to. All believers are of the age to come. We are sons and daughters of the Resurrection and have died to this world and the present evil age. We are all in Christ, and He is "the same yesterday and today and forever" (Hebrews 13:8). "The old things have passed away. Behold, all things have become new" (2 Corinthians 5:17, KJV). Whether we are twenty or eighty, we are all born again of the same imperishable spiritual seed and are anointed by the same Holy Spirit by which we are also led. By one Spirit, we are all baptized into one Body.

Compared to all this, the slight differences of style and technology with which believers of different age groups have been raised are insignificant and superficial. Only church leaders who are unacquainted with the radical transforming power of Christ within the believer and the true power of the anointing of the Holy Spirit are focused on such trivialities.

It's truly time for us twenty-first century American Christians to repent of our cleverness and idolatry to marketing and rediscover God's power to build His church. If we truly want to win the lost, we must do so the same way the early church did. The answer today is the same as back then. They did it through the power of the Holy Spirit and by demonstrating love and reconciliation. This must be our way today.

Enlarge Your Circle of Love

We must become a spiritual family. We must become a refuge of safety, healing, and preparation. Young people today need the protection and care of a family. This is lacking for so many. Some time ago as I was walking into our lobby before our first Sunday service, I saw David, a thirteen-year-old neighborhood boy who is being raised by a single mother. He looked unkempt and tired. I asked him how he was. He replied, "Last night my mother never came home. I sat up all night worried and afraid. I jumped at every sound. But then I realized that it was Saturday night, and if I could just hang on until the morning I could come to church and everything would be all right."

I do not know what will become of David. I do not know how his future will turn out. I do not know if he will be able to overcome all the problems and difficulties he has encountered growing up. I have learned that there are no guarantees about the kids that we invite into our spiritual family. I do know that on that day at least, we were a place of refuge and safety to him. I do know that we are offering him something that he would not have a chance at otherwise. We are offering him a place in a family, our family. I know that on that Sunday at least, we were the church Jesus wants us to be.

The Joshua Principle

12

Conversions That Stick

Part One
Understanding God's Diagnosis

A nyone who has been in youth ministry for long will tell you that, although it's relatively easy to get a young person to make a commitment to Christ, the failure rate after several years is very high. To a degree, some of this is to be expected. After all, the youngsters making the commitments are not yet mature, nor do they have tested integrity. In addition, the period of adolescence is very turbulent, and our society puts powerful temptations in our kids' way. We should not be shocked or overly discouraged by the frequent spiritual failure—hopefully only temporary—of the kids we are helping.

Part of the fault is also ours. Often our strategies to bring these kids to spiritual maturity are one dimensional and inadequate. Too often a church's youth ministry is entirely comprised of entertaining the kids and then giving them inspiring messages that bring the kids to the altar for yet one more recommitment. But bringing our kids to spiritual maturity requires much more than entertaining and inspiring them. It also requires nurturing, healing, equipping, educating, discipling, and activating them.

In order to bring our kids to strong, tested maturity, we must understand the steps that are required. We can't expect to

133

be successful if we don't understand the process, but just what is the process? What strategy is best? What issues must be addressed? What methods should we employ? These are important questions. Having watched many hundreds of youngsters stumble and fall in their Christian life over three decades (although many later returned with a stronger faith), I have struggled and prayed much over this question. One day as I was reading the Bible, God gave me the answer. *He showed me a before and after picture of a believer.* Just like those weight-loss advertisements we have all seen, it showed a dramatic change. But unlike those pictures, this one showed what was on the inside. It was actually an x-ray or a schematic of the unregenerate person. By studying it we find the strategy to bringing any person, including youth, to maturity in Christ. The picture I am referring to is in the Book of Colossians.

*And although you were **formerly** alienated and hostile in mind, engaged in evil deeds, **yet He has now** reconciled you in His fleshly body through death, in order to present you before Him holy and blameless and beyond approach.*

Colossians 1:21-22, emphasis mine

We all recognize that verse 22 is the picture of what God wants to bring forth in the believer's life: "reconciled... holy and blameless and beyond approach." This is where we all want to get to. Our Christian life is a journey toward these characteristics, which Jesus will work out in our lives by His grace. This is the *after* picture.

Three Battlegrounds

We see the *before* picture in verse 21. It gives us a schematic of the unregenerate person or brand-new, carnal believer. We learn that

134

they are marked by three things. They are "alienated and hostile in mind, and engaged in evil deeds." This is a clear diagnosis of the problem. It shows us what we must address. It describes the natural state of every person outside of Christ Jesus, what we call our "old nature." This is what makes it so hard for people to live the Christian life consistently and why so many backslide. Even after a person is born again, their old nature continues to pull at them. To bring them to maturity, their "old nature" or "old self" must be increasingly overthrown by their "new self." *This diagnosis also gives us our strategy.* It shows us the three primary arenas in which we must operate to help any person overcome the old carnal life and become a spiritual person. The term *"hostile in mind"* refers to **their thinking,** *"alienated"* to **their affections** and *"engaged in evil deeds"* to **their habits and lifestyles.**

Hostile in Mind

We learn that they are "hostile in mind." This speaks of their *thinking and worldview.* This was certainly true of the Greeks that Paul was writing to. They had been raised in a culture marked by paganism, polytheism, Greek philosophy, and sexual immorality. Their natural mind had been fortified against God's truth. But it's just as true of young people in America today.

For the vast majority who attend public school, they have been trained and educated in doubt, unbelief, and humanism since they were five years old. Therefore, doubt and unbelief come easily to them, but faith does not. They are educated in a place where the word "God" can seldom, if ever, even be voiced and the Bible can never be referred to in an authoritative way in any discussion about anything. Therefore, God seems unreal and the Bible begins to lose its authority in their lives.

135

Youth who have been so educated may want to believe in all of the stories of the Bible and have a deep trust in God, but their *hostile* mind keeps tripping them up. Biblical beliefs are forever being undermined by the worldview and views they have been taught. Biblical assumptions, moral standards and beliefs that seemed reasonable and obvious to those raised in previous American generations are now met with skepticism and opposition of a mind formed by our education system and popular media.

To say that they are "hostile in mind" means that they have been given a worldview that is full of prejudice against God and His ways, and that is anti-Bible. Even after a person has an encounter with God and makes a commitment to Him, they can still have a mind full of ideas hostile to God and His ways. These are false beliefs and standards that will color how they evaluate and make decisions about things like sex, their relationship to authority, their self-image, their view of ethics and morality, etc. An unbiblical viewpoint on these areas will cause them to backslide and fall short of God's plan for them. The arguments and reasoning of men will hold them captive, unable to fully move forward into the freedom and blessing God has for them. Paul warned these same Christians.

See to it that no one takes you captive through philosophy and empty deception, according to the tradition of men....

Colossians 2:8

When young people look at today's media and sit in today's classrooms, they are presented with a world that doesn't include God. He is not included in the explanation of anything, nor does He factor in the discussion of anything. It's as if He doesn't exist.

Famous economist F.F. Schumacher tells of a trip he took years ago to the Soviet Union. While in St. Petersburg, known as Leningrad during most of the Soviet period, he decided to see the sites of the city. After a few hours he became lost. He found a huge Russian Orthodox church near the middle of town. Built many years before the atheistic communists took power, it dominated the skyline and could be seen for many blocks. He decided that he could find his position on the map that his communist host and tourism official had given him by locating this huge church. Try as he might, he could not find this huge and historic church on the map. Later, after finding his way back to his host's home, he asked him about it. His host replied; "Oh, we don't ever show churches on our maps." The atheistic communists pretended that these massive, magnificent churches weren't there even though everyone could see them. The experience struck him as very odd and later he wrote these words, "I realized that this wasn't the first time I had been given a map which failed to show me what was right before my eyes. All through school and then university I had been given maps of life and knowledge on which there was hardly a trace of many of the things which were of greatest importance."

For the last forty-five years, due to several Supreme Court decisions, all public education has excluded the Bible, reference to God, and His importance in the founding of our nation. Following that lead, popular entertainment and media have increasingly done the same. God has been removed from the maps we give our kids. It's as though He doesn't exist and never did except in the folk beliefs of superstitious, old fashioned people. It's as though "science" has somehow disproved God.

A person can't live for long behaving contrary to how they perceive reality. If they believe that the scientific evidence suggests that God doesn't exist, they will forever be plagued with doubts about Him. If they are taught it's unreasonable to ask a person to deny themselves any sexual pleasure and limit sex to the marriage bed, then they will not be able to remain sexually pure. If they have a humanistic view of authority and the absolute freedom of the individual, then they will not grant spiritual leaders authority over them.

All of these positions will lead to very harmful consequences. In order for people to be brought through to maturity, there must be a comprehensive overhaul of their views and assumptions until those views are biblical. *If kids give their hearts to Jesus but the world still has their minds, then sooner or later they will backslide.*

There is more to their hostile mind than merely what they have been taught by education and culture. Sin also plays a part in forming their views. You see, as we grow up, people's sinful actions against us begin to affect our view of the world. Complicating the problem are the sinful responses of our own heart to the wrong actions of others. Bitterness, fear, and cynicism come to poison our thinking and perspective. Our own pride can begin to build walls that blind and prejudice us as well.

Many young people grow up angry at God, blaming Him for what others have done. Others feel unlovable. They have been rejected by man and can't believe that God really loves them. The natural mind, because it has been bent and twisted by the abuse of others along with the effects of our own pride and sin, does not easily accept God's Word.

The natural mind is full of untrue ideas about God. It has a warped view of reality. It often responds in a hostile fashion to what God says in the Bible. It mistrusts Him and His commands. Often this can lead to a mistrust and rejection of all adults and authority figures. One of the hardest people I ever worked with was a young person named Paul. He had been abandoned by both parents. He grew up in several foster homes and group homes and was abused.

He told me that one day he swore never to trust an adult again. This became a stronghold in his mind. You can imagine the devastation it brought into his life. It takes patience, love, and skill in God's Word to help straighten out a hostile mind.

This means that we must take the content of what we teach our youth seriously. We must replace a humanistic worldview with a theistic worldview. We must replace sinful, self-defeating thinking with God's Word. Yes, our teaching ministry to our kids must be interesting and engaging, but it must not be shallow. It must be comprehensive and convincingly taught. We must do more than entertain and inspire our kids. We must give them a systematic curriculum that covers all the questions that they are asking. The very questions that trained secularists—and even the devil—are answering them wrongly. Questions like: *How did the world get here? How should I think about the fact that other people believe in different religions? How can I know what is right and wrong? Can I really trust God? How can I be sure that He loves me? How should I handle my newly emerging sexuality?*

At our church we try to meet this need in a variety of ways. Our mentoring program includes a curriculum we wrote that builds a biblical foundation and worldview for the youth's self-concept, relationship to authority, ethics and sexuality, and other topics. These are available from our website.[17] In addition, we offer seminars and workshops on these and other topics at our camps and annual youth conference. We also hold an annual "worldviews institute" that we call North Star, which is especially targeted to those who are attending college or graduating from high school. Our church's elementary, middle, and high school all stress worldview training in their curriculum as well.

---

[17] http://YVCenters.com (May 15, 2007).

Our kids are asking important questions. We must help them to find the answers. This is one reason why ministry to our youth can't merely be left to temporary, unqualified, and unprepared workers. This is why we must pay our youth ministers the same as any other associate pastor, because we need to attract our very best people to this job. The competition for the minds of young people today is intense, and we need gifted, trained, educated, and self-motivated people to head up this ministry. As we have seen, this is the critical battleground for the future of the church and our nation. It's a great sin to bore kids with the Bible. We must make our teaching interesting and relevant. We should use illustrations and object lessons and good preparation. We can't just throw something together. We must *deserve* to be heard. If a church isn't large enough to hire such a person, then the senior pastor must directly oversee this ministry as one of his primary duties.

Another important way we can accomplish this is by supporting the efforts of home-schooling parents. Many churches, like ours, have home-school family groups that work together to help each other.

Additionally, churches should start and support Christian schools. This is an expensive proposition, especially at the high school level, but one that we can accomplish by working together and remembering that the church of tomorrow will depend upon the kids we raise up today, not the buildings that we build. The future of the church depends upon the church of today having the right priorities.

Alienated

The next thing we learn about young people who come to Christ is that they are "alienated." This speaks of their affections. Not only are the unregenerate mind and heart not inclined toward pleasing God, but young people are being raised in a culture that makes God and the Bible out to be unreal and unappealing. On the other hand it makes sin, unbelief, and rebellion seem normal and appealing. As a result, kids develop an appetite and taste for worldly things but not for godly things. This is, of course, truer of those raised in unchurched homes than for those raised in churched homes, but it's true of everyone. Spiritual things, or the things of God, seem alien and strange to the natural man, especially one raised with popular American entertainment and culture.

We have many aliens living in America. Some are here for a short period, perhaps for schooling or training, some for longer periods. What we notice about them is that they prefer the music, food, sports, customs, and even language of their previous culture. Their tastes, views, and interests were developed there while young. Our ways seem alien and unappealing to them. Some of our customs and views may even seem incomprehensible to them. They are alienated from our culture and ways. They are not familiar or comfortable with them.

Most young people today who come to church feel like aliens. While they may have an inner spiritual hunger, the culture that they are raised in has given them little appetite for God's ways described in the Bible. When we talk about the value of humility, the beauty of holiness, the joy of moral purity, or servanthood, they stare blankly. Our popular culture does not value these things. In fact, it portrays them in a very negative light. Culture has a profound shaping influence on the tastes, affections, and behaviors of those who grow up in them.

Have you ever noticed how most British are very polite, quiet, and reserved and that they like to eat fish and chips and play cricket? On the other hand, Australians are very loud, bold, even brash, and like to eat meat pies and play Rugby. What explains this difference? Is it genetics? Of course not, since so many of the Australians trace their origin to England. The correct answer is culture. Take two twins and have one raised in Australia and one in England. You will end up with one Australian and one Brit. Their tastes, fashions, preferences, and loyalties will conform to the culture they were raised in. That is the power of culture.

Unless a young person is raised in a very healthy and devout family that exercises wise and loving oversight of him, and unless he also attends a healthy, vibrant evangelical church actively and is either home-schooled or attends a Christian school, then it's likely that he's shaped by the dominant popular culture of America. That culture has alienated him from biblical Christianity.

If we are going to see these young people brought to spiritual maturity, we are going to have to deal with this whole problem of alienation. We are going to have to deal with their affections. We have to make what now seems abnormal to them seem normal and what now seems incomprehensible to them understandable and reasonable. We will have to help make appealing to them what the culture has made unappealing. In short, we have to overcome their alienation and bring them into the culture of God. If we do this, they will be more likely to finish their course.

How do we do this? In order to be successful, we must do two things. First, we must oversee and restrict their involvement in a hostile culture that produces alienation from the ways of God. And second, we must do something positive. We must put something in the place of the things we are taking away. We do this by inviting them to experience a new culture. We offer them love and a new circle of peers and friends. We give them new role models that will love them and whom they can respect. This new culture, infused as it is with the power and love of the Holy Spirit, will begin to reshape their affections and loyalties.

This does not just happen automatically because you want it to or because you gather all your young people together under one roof for one hour a week. Rather, it's something that you must plan and strategize.

Fun and Games?

Sometimes you hear adult leaders complain about all the fun and games and socializing that are associated with youth ministry. Sometimes they will say things like, "Why can't we just get into the Word?" But this ignores an important aspect of helping our young people to become disciples. In order for us to overcome their alienation, we will have to help them form new friends and win their affections.

If all we do is assault their minds without winning their hearts, we will not be very successful. We'll find they don't lend us their ears but instead protect them from what we are saying. And even if we do get through and convince their minds, if their affections are still alienated, and if they have not made new friends, it will be only a matter of time before they succumb to their old ways. This is because, much more than for adults, their thinking follows their affections. They listen to the people they like.

For this reason, helping them to form a social network of Christian friends is vitally important. One way that we do this is by structuring ministry projects and exciting events that are likely to build friendships. Think about it; when you were in junior high and high school, your friends were probably those whom you played with on a team, worked with on a project like a school play or a school newspaper, or had adventures with like surf trips and motorcycle races. These are the times when lasting friendships are formed. We try to get our kids to work together on various ministry projects and also schedule camps, trips, and special events that will form the kind of memories that bond people together.

Today, we have lots of weddings at our church among our young adults, and very often their wedding party is primarily formed out of people that they went to camps with and did ministry with beginning in junior high. They formed the most important and influential friendships of their lives there. I watch as they have children and raise them together.

One of our greatest challenges in dealing with the problem of alienation is in our Youth Venture outreach program. According to our surveys, more than 90 percent of these kids come from homes that are not involved with a church. When they walk in that door the first time, many of them have never been inside a church or ever read even one chapter of the Bible. In the majority of cases, at least one parent—almost all are divorced—has a problem with drugs or alcohol, and most of these parents have unbiblical worldviews and lifestyles. Most of these kids have few if any friends who are even nominal Christians. *In other words, these kids are highly alienated.*

One of the first things that we do with them is to take them on a two-day trip to Magic Mountain which is a four-hour drive away. It's the first incentive trip or reward that they qualify for once they have completed three mentoring sessions. These trips are a mix of brand-new members along with long-time members who have now become solid Christians. Since Youth Venture works primarily with disadvantaged kids, many of these new kids have never been that far away from home before. Most have never been to Magic Mountain.

Being with 150 others from Youth Venture overnight in a motel along with two days at the theme park is a memorable adventure for most of them. Strong friendships begin to form.

In addition, we take them on beach camps where we teach them to surf, as well as camping trips, fishing trips, leadership camps, mission trips, service projects, and other memory-making events. Through these they begin to form new relationships with people who become their primary friends. These replace the wrong friends that they were choosing before. This strategy is essential to our success with them, and it works. We hear it over and over again in their testimonies.

In addition, our adult mentors introduce them to various other experiences and events that begin to give them a taste of Christian culture and healthy family life. Slowly but surely their affections and tastes change. What seems normal and preferable to them changes. Gradually they begin to develop an appetite for righteousness, worship, Bible study, ministry, and service. These are spiritual appetites that before had never been stimulated or allowed to develop.

Engaged in Evil Deeds

This last problem deals with lifestyle, including such things as habits and even addictions. Many youth today are taking the first steps into very ungodly, negative lifestyles and beginning to form dangerous habits and addictions. One very important component of all of these is their use of time. Time must be invested in order for something to become a lifestyle or a habit. Wrong habits and wrong lifestyles result from investing time in wrong things. One reason young people become ensnared by drugs, drinking, dangerous Internet relationships, or even gangs is because they have an abundance of unsupervised time that they begin to invest in these destructive activities. *Thus, their use of time is the third arena in which we must have a strategy if we are to see young people mature in Christ.*

In order for a wrong habit, lifestyle, or addiction to be overcome, the time that was invested in that behavior must be invested in something new and different. If we are to help young people come to maturity in Christ, we are going to have to help them with new ways to spend their time.

In the ideal family, Mom and Dad take care with how their children spend their time and closely monitor what activities they are involved in. Most important, they make sure that plenty of time is reserved for meaningful family interaction. However, the great majority of kids growing up today are not growing up in the ideal family. Unfortunately, this is true even in the church, and even more so in our outreach to the community. In fact, many of the youth who will visit or attend church events and programs are latch-key kids who spend many hours each week without any real supervision.

One hour on Sunday morning and two hours at Wednesday night youth group is not sufficient. We must offer more support to our youth than this. We must structure more time for our youth that is positive and supervised. Our experience shows us that there is a huge amount of youth, even among the unchurched, that will choose to do something positive, supervised, and safe if they are given the chance. This is true for many of those who are beginning to dabble in dangerous and sinful behavior as well.

As an example of this, our Youth Venture Teen Centers are open seven days a week and are usually full of kids who are choosing to try and stay out of trouble. Many of these youth will visit these centers three to seven days a week for a period of years. As you can imagine, it's not the pool tables or arcade games that keep them coming back. All that stuff would grow old after several months. What they are looking for is family and a safe place. Youth Venture is that safe place. It offers adult supervision and structure away from the temptations and pressures of the street and school campus. In addition to that, our thirteen Higher Ground Christian Clubs also help encourage our students and, like the teen centers, build a positive peer group for them. These after school clubs operate at all thirteen middle schools that are near our Youth Venture Teen Centers, as do our ten elementary school Bible clubs.

I believe that it's spiritual child abuse to lead a young person to Christ and tell them to lead a pure and holy life and then abandon them to the culture of the street, the campus, and the entertainment media. It's wrong to urge our children to live by Christian standards and then abandon them to places where they are almost certain to fail. Left to themselves, the great majority of young teens don't have the self-confidence and inner fortitude to withstand the daily pressure and temptations they face. Consequently, most young Christians today are starting off with a foundation of compromise and spiritual failure. Those who should become the leaders of the church of tomorrow are learning to settle for defeat and compromise.

Part of the strategy to win and disciple the next generation for Christ must involve the whole issue of the free time of young people. We can't just talk about quality time but also quantity time. In fact, if we won't invest a large quantity of time in young people, we will find that the time we do have with them will not be quality time. This is because it takes time to form meaningful relationships, and this is especially true when speaking of adolescents.

The most important way that you communicate love to adolescents is by giving them the gift of your time. It seems that, at this age, they spell love T-I-M-E. They are looking for people who will spend time with them and help them explore a new world that is opening up to them. They are seeking fun and new experiences, and they are hungering for people who will travel the road with them. As much as they may love their parents, they are looking outside the home for new relationships and safe, ordered places to go. *They are looking for people who can help them interpret this new life that they are being thrust into.*

Something important and profound takes place when you just hang out with kids.

Relationships are formed, and trust is developed. There is no such thing as "down time" when you are with them. It's all important time. Danny Eslinger, who is director of our Youth Venture Centers and Higher Ground Clubs, told me, "The biggest thing I have learned from my eight years with Youth Venture and Higher Ground Clubs is the importance of spending lots of time with the kids, of spending and sharing your life with them over their highs and lows."

But how can we hang out with kids? Sometimes it can be as simple as spontaneously taking them out for a soda and a pizza. But to be effective we must plan it. Planning camping and fishing trips, involving youth in ministry and short-term missions teams, building a youth hang-out center, or participating in a Christian sports league are all ways to help young people hang out with people from church. At our church we have done all of these and more. **Yes, it requires time and effort, but if your church doesn't have enough time for children and youth, then your priorities are wrong. Go back and reprioritize what you are doing.**

Apart from the family, the church must become the center of the young person's social life if we are to help them to change and mature. We must make the church community a place where they want to be and want to spend lots of time. Our goal at Foothills is that our young people find their best friends at church. We also want them to form at least four or five important relationships with non-family adults at our church. We structure events and adventures to help these goals to take place. Not every church will do it like ours; not every church could do what we do. But God has an answer for every praying church on how to help their young people in this third arena, the arena of time.

Strategize for Success

These are the three arenas that we must strategize in to be successful. We must help young people in the area of their thinking, affections, and use of time. Today, we have hundreds of young disciples from the ages of middle school to college walking in Christian maturity and serving Christ. They have gone out not only in our own community but across America and even around the world. One reason for this is that we have read God's diagnosis of the problem in the first chapter of Colossians and strategized accordingly.

It's important to realize that you will not be successful if you work at only two of the three arenas. For instance, if you work hard to have lots of inviting and entertaining programs to win the kids' hearts and keep them busy but do not provide answers to life's questions or help them to form a Christian worldview, they will either fall away or become nominal Christians at best. Likewise, if you keep them busy with lots of classes that give them lots of information but do not win their affections, then they are likely to simply tune you out and listen to someone else who has their heart. Finally, if you send them to the best, most exciting camps with the best speakers on earth twice a year but do not have something for them several times a week in between those camps, they will soon backslide. The day will come when you won't even be able to get them to go to the camps.

God tells us the problem is they are "alienated and hostile in mind, and engaged in evil deeds." Only by addressing all three arenas will we see the results that we pray for. The reaction of some churches may well be that this will require too much effort. Such churches don't get it. This is exactly where our effort and finances *must* be spent. This is the decisive battleground. We simply must succeed at this even if it means that we rethink and reprioritize what we're doing. Some churches may have to share resources and volunteers to be effective, but we must, at all costs, be effective. We cannot, we dare not, fail with our children and youth.

13

Conversions That Stick

Part Two
Understanding God's Cure

As we have just seen, the first chapter of Colossians gives us a diagnosis of the human condition apart from Christ. It shows why it's hard for people to walk with God and why so often new converts backslide. *In our natural state we are* "alienated and hostile in mind, and engaged in evil deeds." But that same chapter, only seven verses later, gives us our strategy for bringing our young people to spiritual maturity. It shows us how to go from the before picture to the after picture.

> We **proclaim** Him, **admonishing** every man and **teaching** every man with all wisdom, so that we may present every man complete in Christ. For this purpose also I **labor,** striving according to His power, which mightily works within me.
>
> Colossians 1:28-29, emphasis mine

In this verse Paul gives us the strategy to bring young people, or anyone for that matter, to maturity in Christ. He says his goal is to "present every man complete in Christ" (verse 28). This is the "after" picture that was, as you will remember, defined six verses earlier as "holy and blameless and beyond reproach" (Colossians 1:22).

Just as this chapter gives us the diagnosis of the problem, it

151

also gives us God's prescription and treatment plan. We cannot expect to get God's results unless we follow His plan. Note that there are four root verbs given to us. They are: *proclaim, admonish, teach,* and *labor.* These four words hold the key to seeing transformation take place in another person. Only by following this exact plan will we be able to "present" a person "complete in Christ." This is important to stress. There are a great many humanistic and psychological ideas in the church about how to help our kids. However, God is clear about His method and plan. Experience has shown that only His way brings about His results.

Proclaim

The first part of our fourfold strategy is contained in the words, "we proclaim Him."

This refers, of course, to proclaiming or preaching Jesus Christ. Jesus is God's answer to the human problem. He is the total solution to every young person's problem and need, but we must present Jesus in His fullness. All of our ministry must be built upon a clear proclamation of Jesus as Savior, Lord, Teacher, and Christ (Baptizer in the Holy Spirit). These are the four main titles given Jesus in the New Testament because these are the four roles or offices that Jesus occupies.

If we neglect any of these aspects of Jesus' ministry in our procla- mation of Him, we present only a partial Jesus, and thus only a partial solution to people's problems. He is only able to save them from the problems of this life (Savior) if they follow His directions and commands (Lord). He brings them into a life of freedom only as they learn His principles and truths (Teacher). Yet they will only be able to overcome sin, devastation, and the power of the devil through receiving and walking in the power of the Holy Spirit (Christ).[18] Only by leading our young people into embracing Jesus in all four of His roles will they know true freedom and victory. I have written extensively of this in my book *On Earth as It Is in Heaven.*

I will only say that any ministry that truly brings about transformation must be built first and foremost upon proclaiming Christ as the total solution. Simply showing a young person unconditional love, trying to build up their self-esteem, or giving them psychological counseling will not bring about true transformation. Only Jesus will bring spiritual transformation and a changed life, and only if He is proclaimed in all four of His roles.

As I have stated in this book, there are many things that we can do to help kids to change and grow, but they are all useless if Christ is not clearly proclaimed and if the young person will not accept Him and yield to Him. There is no other foundation on which to build (1 Corinthians 3:11). It seems that some sectors of the church have lost confidence in proclaiming Christ. They try to help young people using humanistic means, but I can assure you that Jesus is the only answer and that young people are hungry for Him and will respond to Him even when they won't respond to anything else.

Proclaiming Christ is self-authenticating. By that I mean that the Holy Spirit will bear witness as well. When you proclaim Christ clearly and in the right spirit, then the Holy Spirit will Himself bear witness within the person you are speaking to (John 16:8). Even if He does not seem to at that very moment, be certain that He will at the right moment. I believe and have become absolutely convinced of the power of bearing witness to Christ Jesus. Jesus is the only answer to people's deepest needs.

---

[18]Christ is a transliteration of the Greek word meaning "Anointed One." This refers to Jesus ministry of baptizing in the Holy Spirit. John the Baptist said, "I baptized you with water; but He will baptize you with the Holy Spirit" (Mark 1:8).

Admonish

The Greek word translated "admonish" is the word *noutheteo*. It comprises both the meaning of warning and instruction. That is, we point out to people the consequences for their wrong actions and instruct them in a better way. Part of bringing people into the deliverance and freedom of Christ is calling them to repentance. Many young people are headed for real heartbreak and tragedy if they don't change their attitudes and behavior. It may be true that some of their attitudes and behavior are rooted in what others have done to them or failed to do. In some cases the abandonment, neglect, mistreatment, or abuse may have been quite severe. So we must show them it's their own present attitudes and actions that will cost them in the future. We must lead them to take responsibility for what they're presently doing. We must help them to see that they, not their parents or anyone else, will determine what their future will be like.

Had we the time, I could contrast the lives of many, many young people. Although all of them come from similar backgrounds, some accepted the love and help offered, made good choices, and went on to happy and productive lives. Others let their lives be determined by their circumstances. They made no proactive decisions but became passive victims.

While learning of the difficulties of a young person's life may give us great compassion and patience for them, we cannot let it become an excuse for their continuing in wrong attitudes and actions. Remember, God can heal any wound and redeem any tragedy, but He cannot bless rebellion or unrighteousness. They must come to believe that whatever their past, Jesus is able to reward them for faithful, obedient actions today. We must teach them patience since the reward of acting rightly is not always immediate, but it is always certain. We must be willing to stand with them and strengthen them during times when their resolve is being tested.

The truth is that obedience is always blessed by God, but sin, unbelief and rebellion inevitably bring about negative consequences. We do young people no favor by sugarcoating it or refusing to confront them where they are wrong. This, of course, must be done at the proper time and as the Lord leads. This is what is meant by the words "admonishing...and teaching...with all wisdom." We must respond to the Lord's wise leading, not our impatience, frustration, or anger if we want our admonishing to be successful. Scripture directs us to be sure that we understand the situation fully before we admonish someone and that we do so in love and humility.

He who gives an answer before He hears, it is folly and shame to him.
Proverbs 18:13

There is one who speaks rashly like the thrusts of a sword, but the tongue of the wise brings healing.
Proverbs 12:18

But everyone must be quick to hear, slow to speak and slow to anger; for the anger of man does not achieve the righteousness of God.
James 1:19-20

When we express love toward the kids, and lead them to experience the love and goodness of God, then they begin to open up to receive our correction or admonishment. Our first job is to embody the love of God and lead them to experience the mercy of Christ, but this honeymoon with Jesus will be short lived if they do not begin to alter their behavior or attitudes to honor Christ.

155

Teach

Teaching is different from admonishing. Whereas admonishing has mainly to do with correction and retraining, teaching is more positive. Teaching is preparing them with God's principles for the challenges and opportunities they will encounter in the future. Teaching is more forward looking. Teaching will enable them to avoid pitfalls and benefit from opportunities.

The goal of our teaching is to prepare our young people with wisdom. Wisdom may be defined as the knowledge and skill to succeed in life through making right choices. No one is born with wisdom. It must be acquired. The Bible calls the elders to teach wisdom to the young.

In the Book of Proverbs the young are frequently referred to as "the naïve" (Proverbs 1:4 and 7:7). The term *naïve* is a good one for youth. It means they are unprepared and lack judgment and experience. Too often the result is tragedy.

For the waywardness of the naïve will kill them.
                                                    Proverbs 1:32

A prudent [wise] man sees evil and hides himself, the naïve proceed and pay the penalty.
                                                    Proverbs 27:12

The naïve inherit folly [i.e. the consequences of foolishness].
                                        Proverbs 14:18, NASB 77

Many young people are facing life unprepared. Therefore, they're easily led into foolish choices and harm. Choices made during this time often plague them for the rest of their lives with terrible consequences. Yet wisdom would allow them to avoid the pitfalls and begin their adult life with a good start.

One of the great difficulties of being young today is that little preparation is given them for what they'll have to face. Many grow up without the presence and counsel of a father in the home. Others have parents in the home who are preoccupied with their own problems, like drugs, alcohol, interpersonal, financial, or work problems. They are either unavailable emotionally to their kids or they lack wisdom themselves. Even in the church many young people are growing up in dysfunctional homes where wisdom seems in short supply.

When these same young people go outside the home, wisdom can still be hard to find. The philosophy of the day is humanistic relativism where absolute truth is denied and moral judgments are frowned on.

The result is that our young people do not know how to play the game of life. They don't even know what the rules are. God's directions for the game have been hidden from them. How can they win? They are frustrated and hungry for answers and directions. We who know and believe the Bible can give them the wisdom that they need to succeed in life. The Bible alone can fully equip them and make them adequate for any challenge that life will throw at them.

From childhood you have known the sacred writings which are able to give you the wisdom that leads to salvation through faith which is in Jesus Christ. All Scripture is inspired by God and profitable for teaching, for reproof, for correction, for training in right-eousness; so that the man of God may be adequate, equipped for every good work.

2 Timothy 3:15-17

Only as we put the Scripture at the center of our ministry to kids will we be able to see them become mature Christians, fully equipped and adequate to be more than conquerors in life. Then they will be fully prepared to succeed.

The Place of God's Word

I can't stress enough the futility of trying to minister to young people without putting the Word of God at the center of your strategy. It's only the Word of God that will correct and build up young believers and bring them God's riches. The Apostle Paul, when saying goodbye to the Ephesian elders for the last time, knew what their future success depended upon.

*And now I commend you to God and to **the word of His grace, which is able to build you up and to give you the inheritance** among all those who are sanctified.*

Acts 20:32, emphasis mine

Several years earlier Paul had left Timothy in charge of that same Ephesian church with this charge:

*Until I come, **give attention to the public reading of Scripture, to exhortation and teaching. Do not neglect the spiritual gift within you,** which was bestowed upon you through prophetic utterance with the laying on of hands by the presbytery. **Take pains with these things; be absorbed in them,** so that your progress will be evident to all. Pay **close attention to yourself and your teaching;** persevere in these things, for as you do this **you will ensure salvation** both for yourself and for those who hear you.*

1 Timothy 4:13-16, emphasis mine

Paul's counsel and direction to Timothy and to the Ephesian elders is just as relevant to us today. In order for any ministry to

158

bear lasting fruit, Spirit-led, and inspired proclamation and instruction in God's Word must be central. When I honor God's Word I honor God. When I boldly teach and proclaim His Word I throw the ministry squarely onto His shoulders. To the extent I won't put teaching His Word at the center of my strategy, I take responsibility away from Him and place it on myself. To that extent I limit the results to what I can accomplish instead of what He could do. Any strategy to help kids must put proclaiming and teaching the Word of God as a top priority.

Labor

The fourth key strategic word in this passage is the word "labor." Consider this, which Paul wrote in another place:

> *For this purpose also I labor, striving according to His power, which mightily works within me.*
> Colossians 1:29

Paul knew what was required, and he was willing to pay the price and do whatever it took. He knew that the battle could not be won without striving and laboring. He also knew that human strength would be insufficient. He relied on the power of God.

If we want to see young people won to Christ and established as strong Christians it will take great effort and great wrestling. There will be a high demand in financial and human resources. This is where the battle is most intense. The battle for the souls of the next generation is the greatest struggle on earth. It will not be easily won. Nor will it be won by our own strength and cleverness.

Youth leaders, please hear me. The great need of the hour is not for greater innovation but for greater anointing. It's not another seminar that you need. What you need is the power of God.

You will not get that searching the Internet but rather crying out to God on your knees. There is nothing that will drive me to my knees quicker or with greater desperation than simply taking a look at the dire situation of the younger generation growing up around us. Quite simply, if you really love young people, you will learn how to really pray.

Don't fall into the trap of thinking that the answer is simply more money for youth ministry. No currency on earth can purchase what is needed most. In order to reach this next generation we need more anointing. We need His power to mightily work within us. We need to set aside our breathless pursuit of novelty, innovation, and technique and get a hold of God.

We need to gain the anointing of His Spirit. We need to become people of great prayer. We need to enlist the prayers of others. Every leader should assemble an intercessory prayer team around him. This is a team of people who are committed to praying for his ministry and especially that he will be anointed with more of God's Spirit. But beyond this, we ourselves must pray.

Paul labored and he strove. He put in long hours at times, and he also fought with skill and passion, but he did not do so relying on his own cleverness or talents. He did so relying on the power and gifts of the Holy Spirit.

My message and my preaching were not in persuasive words of wisdom, but in demonstration of the Spirit and of power.
1 Corinthians 2:4

For our gospel did not come to you in word only, but also in power and in the Holy Spirit and with full conviction.
1 Thessalonians 1:5

If we want the results that God promises, then we must follow God's plan. It's a simple plan. It's built upon proclaiming and teaching God's Word in reliance upon the power of God's Spirit. If that seems too simplistic, consider how few ministries today, especially those to young people, are doing it this way. We have become too sophisticated, too prosperous, too tech-savvy, and we have lost our way.

Bringing God's Light and Order Into Darkness and Chaos

Youth culture today is a dangerous place of spiritual darkness and moral chaos. Only God's Word and Spirit can bring order, light, and life to this situation, and the Bible shows us how.

In the first chapter of Genesis we read that the whole earth was covered by a watery, lifeless chaos. Complete darkness was on the surface of the deep waters. Watch how God brings forth order and life.

The earth was formless and void, and darkness was over the surface of the deep, and the Spirit of God was moving over the surface of the waters. Then God said, "Let there be...."

Genesis 1:2-3

Although everything appeared dark, inhospitable and devoid of life, there was something present that could not be seen with human eyes. We read that the Spirit of God was moving or literally "brooding" over the scene. He appeared to be waiting. But waiting for what? And then it came, the very thing He was waiting for—the Word of God. "And God said, 'Let there be....'"

161

With the injection of God's Word, God's Spirit brought forth light, order, and life into the scene. This is God's pattern from the beginning of Creation. He hasn't changed it. When we look out into the darkness and chaos of youth culture, there is something that we can't see with our naked eyes. The Spirit of God is present. He is hovering and brooding. Over every gathering of young people He is brooding, like a hen brooding over its nest. He is ready to bring order, light, and life if we will simply speak the Word of God.

Whenever we go into a new neighborhood to open a new Youth Venture or a new school campus to begin a new Bible club, we know that the Spirit of God is already there. We work hard to build relationships and build bridges, but we know that nothing eternal will happen until we begin to introduce God's Word. Only then will light, order, and life begin to emerge.

Before we open a new Youth Venture Center or begin a new Bible club, we saturate the neighborhood or campus with prayer. We prayer walk the neighborhood and pray over the school. We call upon the Holy Spirit, who is brooding over that neighborhood or campus. Within two weeks of opening a Youth Venture Center we are taking kids through our Scripture-based mentoring lessons. Beginning with our second week at our campus Bible clubs we are teaching the Word of God and teaching the kids to memorize Bible verses. The Spirit is brooding, we introduce the Word, and then lives begin to change. We see young people from the most chaotic and dysfunctional backgrounds begin to change. We see life and order begin to come into the neighborhood and into the school campus. It works because it's God's way.

14

Who Is Qualified?

The answer to the above question is: You are. No matter who you are, you are qualified. You can do something helpful and important in reaching the next generation.

Some time ago I came across the following letter in a local Christian newspaper.

Dear Grandma,

I want you to know that I thank you for your visits, your trust and faith in God, but mostly for believing and being there for me. I want you to know I love you very much and I will thank God for putting you in my life.

I'm not sure where I will be placed up north, but I promise to be good, Grandma, so I can have another chance to better my life. And I'll always keep my faith in God.

I want you to know that you are very special to me. Ever since I met you, you put joy in my heart.

God bless you,
Scott
(seventeen-year-old in Juvenile Hall)

Apparently the newspaper did some research into this letter that was sent to them, because there was an editor's note after the letter.

It stated that Grandma is a volunteer who goes into Juvenile Hall and ministers to the boys and girls. The volunteers are not allowed to give their addresses to the youth that they minister to, and so Scott posted his letter in the Christian newspaper.

It's pretty clear that Grandma must be a somewhat elderly lady to earn that nickname. Most people wouldn't think an old lady could be an effective youth worker, especially with youth delinquents. There was probably a time when God was calling Grandma to this work and she thought, "God, I must be crazy. You wouldn't call me to this. What do I have in common with them? What do I have to offer?"

This is how almost everyone feels. Most feel lost among youth and feel their presence would not be welcome. I remember feeling this way myself when I got started. I remember feeling afraid and expecting rejection. But I found that youth are hungry for adult friendships, encouragement, and counsel.

Could God Use You?

God has a place for every person who has a burden for reaching young people. Every person has something to offer. There is a young person out there who needs you. You are just the right person for that child. You have just what they need. I say this after nearly thirty years of working with children and youth. I say this after seeing hundreds of volunteers of all ages and backgrounds. You have so much more to offer than you realize.

While some adults will feel primarily called to pray and others to support financially—and these are both absolutely vital—never feel that you couldn't also have a very personal role to play in the life of a young person.

Many would disqualify themselves from working with youth. They feel that they are not young enough, pretty enough, funny enough, or exciting enough. The truth is that none of these things hurt, but none of them are necessary either.

Don't fall into the trap of thinking that what kids want most is to be wowed or entertained. Don't think that what they are seeking deep down is for someone to impress them. What they want and need most of all is someone who will accept them, love them, listen to them, and give them direction. If that's you, then you qualify, and you can be successful.

It takes time and patience to get behind the shallow and surface world of our youth and win their trust and touch their hearts, but this is the method and way of Jesus. This is the model He set for us.

God With Us

Jesus became our Savior by first coming down and becoming one of us and living among us. This is known as the Incarnation, which means "in flesh."

And the Word became flesh, and dwelt among us, and we saw His glory, glory as of the only begotten from the Father, full of grace and truth.
John 1:14

BEHOLD, THE VIRGIN SHALL BE WITH CHILD AND SHALL BEAR A SON, AND THEY SHALL CALL HIS NAME IMMANUEL, which translated means "GOD WITH US."
Matthew 1:23

In order to help us, Jesus left His place in heaven and lived among us. He left the perfections of heaven to live in the squalor and hardship of a poor family in Palestine. Israel was a conquered nation, so He lived under the oppression of Roman masters. He was willing to suffer and endure everything that was common to us (Hebrews 2:18; 4:15).

When God wanted to help us, He did not merely drop a tract from heaven. He did more than place an ad, write a book, or start a radio broadcast. He entered our world. He became one of us. He allowed Himself to be misunderstood and mistreated. He came to be Immanuel, "God with us." He sat where we sat and allowed us to put our hands on Him (1 John 1:1).

This is the model Jesus set for us. Really nothing else will work. We too must have an "incarnational ministry." Being incarnational means that we become serious about understanding the world of youth and entering it. This is what Jesus did. If anyone will do what Jesus did, they will be successful.

The Jesus Model of Ministry

Jesus moved from security, strength, and safety to weakness and vulnerability. He left His place, where He was worshiped and all powerful, and came to our place where He was unrecognized and unappreciated. He left heaven, a place unknown and mysterious to us, and came and took on a familiar form and spoke to us in our language. In so doing God became understandable. We could now relate to Him and, therefore, more easily trust Him.

This must be our model. Our adult world seems strange and unapproachable to youth. It's built around our needs and interests, not theirs. It seems as foreign to them as their world does to us. Who will take the initiative to enter the other's world? It must be us since we are the wiser and more mature. We gain credibility when we leave our place and come over to their place and sit where they sit and understand what their life feels like.

To enter the world of children is perhaps not too difficult, but to leave your adult world and enter the world of adolescence requires real sacrifice. For most of us adolescence was not a happy time, and few people are eager to go there again. It's a world where the rules are different. It's a world of confusion and false standards. It's a world that desperately needs adults.

It's a world, however, where the Holy Spirit is quite comfortable. If you offer yourself to Him, He will lead you into it and help you navigate around it and be effective in it. The Holy Spirit is always relevant, and if you allow Him to lead you, you will be relevant as well. You don't have to look or dress like kids; just love them and let the Holy Spirit be your guide.

You enter their world when you ask them questions and really listen in order to understand instead of just shutting them down with premature advice or judgments. You enter their world when you go where they go and participate in what they are interested in even if you lack skill at it. At the very least you can be a spectator. Kids love it when you watch them show off their ability to skate or play soccer. They are hungry for adult approval and encouragement.

Please remember this one thing that I have learned over and over. If you will just try and feel comfortable with them, then they will feel comfortable with you. If you are warm and accepting of them, then they will be warm and accepting of you.

Jesus didn't come for a short visit; He came to stay with us. It only took Him three days to die on the cross for our sins and be resurrected for our justification, but He spent thirty-three years with us. He didn't even begin His ministry of teaching and healing until

He was thirty years of age. He spent time just being with us. Even now He has not left us. Whenever we gather in His name, He is with us (Matthew 18:20). In fact, He still retains His human form in heaven. He sits at the right hand of the Father representing us (Hebrews 7:25). Jesus made a commitment. He is with us to stay.

Redemption is a process that takes time. Jesus knew this. It takes time for people to learn to trust God and let Him change them. This is especially true of young people. It takes young people time to grow up. Becoming mature is not an overnight process. And they do it on their timetable, not ours. The question is: Are we willing to hang in there for the whole process?

Jesus was relational in His ministry. He made relationships that were committed and durable. Although Jesus had a large preaching and teaching ministry, He focused His efforts on twelve men. We read in Mark 3:14, "And He appointed twelve, so that they would be with Him." They lived with Him and shared His life. He got to know them very well. He helped them to face and overcome their problems. Jesus' order of priority is clear from reading the Gospels. His first priority was His relationship with His Father. Next was His ministry to His disciples, and only after that was His ministry to the larger crowds. He spent time with and devoted great energy to these twelve men. He lived His life before them.

Even though the church wants it fast and easy, it doesn't often work that way. Mass evangelism has been shown to be incredibly ineffective. Attempts at mass discipleship are even worse. People don't change en masse; they change one at a time. For our ministry to be successful it must be relational.

Our first task must be to form relationships with the youth. Sometimes people think they are wasting their time unless they are praying with the youth or teaching them the Bible. Sometimes you hear people complain and ask why we spend so much time just hanging out with kids. Well, something happens when you're willing to just "waste your time" with kids. Something profound happens in the relationship when you play football with them or have a shake with them.

You can't skip this process of making relationships. Unlike adults, they're not likely to receive from someone they aren't convinced likes them and whom they like. Kids aren't projects. You can't just impose your agenda on them. But if you'll take the time to form relationships with them, you'll find they'll open up their hearts and lives to you.

Jesus remained committed to the twelve even when they failed and let Him down. The Gospels are full of examples of the failure of the twelve. At times they made Jesus quite frustrated and tried His patience (Mark 9:17-19; 33-37). Yet Jesus never rejected them or gave up on them.

When a young person starts coming to church or goes forward for an altar call, there are no guarantees on how it's all going to go from there. Be prepared for them to disappoint you and let you down. Expect them to be less dependable and consistent than adults. Don't take it personally when they act without integrity. We must be willing to make commitments to young people that take into account the fact that there'll be many failures and disappointments. Some of their wrong choices may persist for weeks, months, and even years. Helping most young people to become mature followers of Christ is a messy affair with lots of ups and downs.

The only guarantee is that they'll be watching you. They'll be watching how you handle their failures, mistakes, and bad choices.

You'll come to be the face of God to them at those times more than any other. An important part of their view of God will be formed at this time. You may be the only constant in their life.

Patience Rewarded

Brett was one of the more difficult youngsters I ever had in my youth group. He would disrupt meetings and provoke people, including me. One time he even spit in my face as a joke. I didn't find it funny. I'd pray to God for patience and try to be compassionate toward him since I knew how bad his background was. I spent extra time with him and grew to like him, although this did not stop him from trying to push my buttons. After about four years he and his mother moved to the beach area. I tried to keep up the relationship as much as possible, but as he got busier and became involved with drugs and partying we lost track of each other.

When he was about twenty-two he showed up at my church one day. He said, "I am working in a church with youth myself now. I want to thank you for all that you taught me and showed me. You will probably never fully appreciate the effect you had on my life." Then he paused for a minute before continuing. "Do you know why I pushed you so hard back when I was in your youth group? It's because every adult in my life was a phony, and nothing they said was ever true. I pushed you because I had to know if what you said was real or not. I had to know if it was really true."

That was fifteen years ago, and he is still in ministry and has a powerful, evangelistic outreach that is reaching many young people. This boy who had been such a trial has now become one of my very close friends. *Some of the greatest impact you will ever have on someone is how you deal with them in their times of failure and foolishness.*

I try to maintain relationships with every young person I have ministered to even when they are living an ungodly lifestyle. I have not changed my home phone number in twenty-five years or my cell phone's in fifteen, so wherever they are, they can find me. On a very regular basis I receive some news, often through a letter, e-mail, or phone call from some young person who used to be involved with me who fell away and wandered off the path. They call to tell me they're back on track and thank me for the investment I made in their lives.

Never give up on people; Jesus doesn't.

The Joshua Principle

Epilogue

By Marc A. Dupont
Mantle of Praise Ministries

By now you realize, after reading *The Joshua Principle,* how vital it is to manifest a commitment to raising up the next generation for Christ, a commitment that goes way beyond a few Bible studies or showing a few videos. It is a commitment of time, energy, and money, as well as a commitment to share with the hurting and lost youth of America the most valuable commodity of all—the commitment of the love of God in your life.

We live in a time and culture offering quick-fix solutions for complex problems. Our instant information age keeps repeating the erroneous message that "If we can simply relate culturally-fun recipes, every problem can be solved." Also, there is the fallback mantra of many ministries who simply declare, "Read your Bible and pray more and it will all work out." Unfortunately, that exhortation is falling flat on the hard, fast track of today's youth culture.

The timeless problem of the need for real relationship within the process of making disciples of Christ is stated in 1 Corinthians 4:15, "You have many teachers but few fathers" (paraphrased). It is easy to find someone who can correctly point out right from wrong, but what kids growing up in a fatherless society need more than anything else is the demonstration of the father heart of God. This takes not only warm bodies and good theology but also involves a long-term commitment to accept, love and nurture those who may be miles away from actually conforming to traditional church culture, behavior, and appearances.

Perhaps the most powerful and poignant part of *The Joshua Principle* is when Mark Hoffman relates the Great Commandment, found in Deuteronomy 6:4-5.

Hear, O Israel! The LORD is our God, the LORD is one! You shall love the LORD your God with all your heart and with all your soul and with all your might.

Combine this with the follow-up in verse 7: *"You shall teach them diligently to your sons."* It is not enough that we adults merely seek to grow in personal godliness, faith, and service to our own generations. We must have God's heart, passion, and commitment for the younger generation today. This generation must experience the reality of the Kingdom of God and His love in a deeply personal way. If not, it will go down the drain of moral abyss simply because, unlike previous generations, there are few tangible examples of biblical absolutes and Judaic/Christian thinking visible in our Western world mainstream cultures.

The last prophet of the Old Testament prophesied of a time when the hearts of the fathers would be restored to the children and the children to the fathers. I believe *The Joshua Principle* is more than a principle, it is a prophetic call to be those future spiritual fathers (and mothers) who respond to the Spirit of God and take His love to a fatherless generation. And, as with the parable Jesus told regarding the Good Samaritan, the question begs to be asked: "Who is the father of the lonely and hurting fatherless in our society?"

It is you and me!

Books by
Mark Hoffman

1. Breakthrough Kingdom Living $10.00
2. On Earth as It Is in Heaven $14.95
3. The Joshua Principle $15.95

You can order these books by filling out the form below, and then enclose your check payable to:

Mark Hoffman
c/o Foothills Christian Church
350 Cypress Lane, Suite B
El Cajon, CA 92020
(619) 442-7728

Or order these books online at: http://shop.foothillschurch.org/

Please rush me: ___book(s) of Book 1 at $10.00 each. ___book(s) of Book 2 at $14.95 each. ___book(s) of Book 3 at $15.95 each.	$_____
I am enclosing $2.95 shipping and handling per book. _____ book(s) x $2.95 each =	$_____
Total enclosed:	$_____

175

The Joshua Principle

Made in the USA
Monee, IL
02 August 2021